Pr 16/4/08

Project-Based Group Work Facilitator's Manual
Young People, Youth Workers and Projects

University of Chester
Warrington Campus

of related interest

Therapeutic Communities for Children and Young People
Edited by Adrian Ward, Kajetan Kasinski, Jane Pooley, Alan Worthington
ISBN 1 84310 096 7
Therapeutic Communities 10

Group Work with Children and Adolescents
A Handbook
Edited by Dr Kedar Nath Dwivedi
Foreword by Robin Skynner
ISBN 1 85302 157 1

Therapeutic Approaches in Work with Traumatized Children
and Young People
Theory and Practice
Patrick Tomlinson
Foreword by Paul van Heeswyk
ISBN 1 84310 187 4
Community, Culture and Change 14

Working with Gangs and Young People
A Toolkit for Resolving Group Conflict
Jessie Feinstein and Nia Imani Kuumba
ISBN 1 84310 447 4

Working with Anger and Young People
Nick Luxmoore
ISBN 1 84310 466 0

Project-Based Group Work Facilitator's Manual
Young People, Youth Workers and Projects

Andy Gibson and Gaynor Clarke

Illustrated by Fiz

Jessica Kingsley Publishers
London and Philadelphia

First published in the United Kingdom in 1995
by Jessica Kingsley Publishers
116 Pentonville Road
London N1 9JB, UK
and
400 Market Street, Suite 400
Philadelphia, PA 19106, USA

www.jkp.com

Library of Congress Cataloging in Publication Data
Gibson, Andy, 1995–
Project based group work facilitator's manual : young people
p. cm
Includes bibliographical references and index.
ISBN 1-85302-169-5 (pbk.)
1. Social work with--Handbooks, manuals, etc. I. Clarke, Gaynor, 1953–
II. Title.
HV1421.G52 1995
362.7--dc20

British Library Cataloguing in Publication Data
Gibson, Andy
Project Based Group Work Facilitator's
Manual: Young People, Youth Workers and Projects
1. Title
361.4

ISBN-13: 978 1 85302 169 5
ISBN-10: 1 85302 169 5

Contents

Part One • The Background

Part Two • Putting it into Practice

Foreword

This book has evolved over a considerable period of time, and as a result we have too many people to thank to list them all here. However, to all of them, and they know who they are, and all the groups we have both had the pleasure of working with, we would like to extend our thanks.

Andy Gibson and Gaynor Clarke both worked together at Sunderland Youth Employment Project between 1982 and 1987. Since then Gaynor has been training apprentice youth and community workers and Andy has been studying and carrying out research. They both have two children, a partner and live in the North East of England.

Fiz, the illustrator, would like to dedicate the cartoons in this book to Lewis Taylor (age 7 1/2), who tested them for funniness, and to Jane Taylor (32 1/4), who provided the inspiration for many of the female characters.

Andy Gibson
Gaynor Clarke

Introduction
...Read This First

This book is about young people, youth workers and projects. Much of youth work practice is devoted to work on projects: big ones, little ones, long ones, short ones, easy ones and hard ones. A project can be anything from organising a trip to the swimming pool to running the youth project itself.

Working with projects is nothing new in youth work, and youth workers have recognised and valued them as an integral part of their work. The benefits to be gained from such work are almost limitless, and one of the problems about developing a coherent practice is that we tend to write about and discuss the purposes and objectives of projects in broad, not easily definable terms such as,

'the development of life and social skills'

'increased self-confidence'

'empowerment'

'citizenship'

'increased abilities'

'developing critical faculties'

'being assertive'

'possessing a coherent value base'

'having a greater awareness'.

These sorts of objectives, it is argued, make 'better people' who are 'more able to make a contribution to their community and society', or are 'able to take control over their lives'.

We take it as read that these are fine ideals; the problem that arises is how to put them into practice: how to ensure that projects become an effective vehicle for these high ideals. How, in the day-to-day difficulties of a youth project, in the hour-to-hour of a youth projects programme and in the minute-to-minute of the youth workers' practice can these hopes be realised? In a similar vein, how can we explain to someone else what we, as youth workers, are trying to do? What do we say when a funder asks why these projects are of value? What do we say when a member of a management committee asks why we don't just run activities in the same way as a leisure centre might? It is sometimes hard to explain the process that leads to these overall aims. Lastly, the gap between our hopes and our projects creates difficulties for us. How can you measure – except in the most vague terms – an increase in 'self-confidence' or 'citizenship' or 'empowerment'? If you cannot do this how can you evaluate and develop your own methods of work, how do you know what works and what doesn't, and how can you make improvements?

Our response to this question is that the only way to work towards these fine ideals, these 'big things', is to identify and understand the smaller details, the momentary incidents that contribute towards them, the 'little things'. Youth workers who set their sights too high are in danger of tripping up on the things close by. The 'big things' we are talking about are, in most cases, over the horizon and we, as youth workers, need landmarks along the way, otherwise how can we know that we are heading in the right direction?

So this book is about those landmarks, those 'little things' that contribute towards our realising the 'big things'. The first part of the book explores what it is we are trying to do; in particular it looks at how skills are learnt, how values, beliefs and understandings are developed and how groups can enhance this process. We also look at how this shapes the role that youth workers play in their work. The second part sets out to see how these things can happen in practice, and explores the methods and techniques youth workers might want to use and develop to bring these fine ideals about. It tries to suggest ways of working that are complementary with the informality, voluntary nature and relative lack of structure of youth projects and centres. We are not suggesting that projects and centres should not be like this, but we are suggesting that the practice needs to compliment these basic features.

Lastly, and most importantly this is not intended to be a prescriptive book. We do not suggest exercises, methods or techniques because they are necessarily right for you, for the groups you work with or for the project you work in. The reason for this is that working with a group is not a science but an art. It is an individual and creative process, and as with any other creative and individual process, one technique, one method, one exercise will not suit everyone. Each person has their own particular style, their own particular approach. Some people are humorous and this shapes their style, some are thoughtful and this shapes their style and some people are by nature quiet, and this shapes the approach they use.

You have to develop a style and approach that suits you and the sort of person you are. This book will not teach you everything about working on projects and it will not solve all your problems, but what it might do is help you develop your style, so you can achieve the ends you have set yourself, and it could help you build up a stock of techniques that you feel comfortable with and help you understand better the things that you are doing anyway.

Some people are humorous and this shapes their style

This book, then, is not an exhaustive collection of exercises and techniques. The suggestions that are made are no more than that: try them if you wish, but there are many more exercises that might suit you, your approach and your style better. You should see this book as

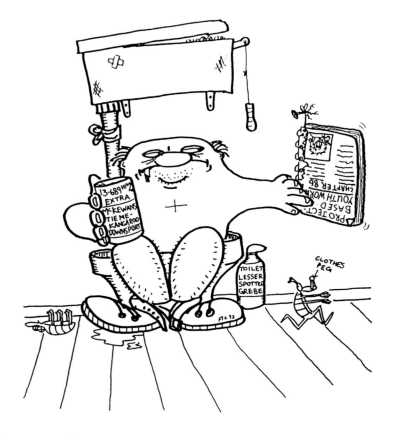

We hope it is of some use to you...

a foundation upon which to build, a rough stone out of which you can carve your own methods and techniques. Throughout we have suggested other books which may contribute further to your practice. Reading these will never be a waste of time, even if you don't always agree with them and the same can be said of talking to colleagues and of any opportunity you have to enter into a dialogue about your practice.

Whatever your approach, we hope it is of some use to you and wish you many happy hours of project based group work.

Andy Gibson
Gaynor Clarke

PART ONE

The Background

1 Skill Development

As we discovered in the introduction, one of the things that we hope young people will gain from youth work is better-developed skills. We also discovered that it is not always clear what is meant by many of these skills. In many ways this does not matter; in fact it may well be the case that there is some benefit to be derived from the fact that youth workers are free to make their own choice about what 'able' means or 'increased self-confidence'. Diversity has always been one of the redeeming features of youth work, but in other ways it is a disadvantage. In practical terms, using concepts like 'able' or 'increased self-confidence' makes it very difficult to put them into practice.

How can a youth worker prepare a session, plan activities or justify their programme to their managers around concepts such as 'able' or 'self-confidence'? What, exactly, do you plan into a programme in order to develop 'citizenship' in young people? How do you prepare a session so that young people become more 'empowered', and how do you explain to a member of a management committee why young people might benefit from a camping weekend which is going to cost four hundred pounds? We don't want to produce clinical definitions that leave no room for spontaneity or creativity, but we do need something a bit better than what we have got. In an attempt to try to break these terms down into manageable terms this book is based on the following twelve 'core skills':

1. **The ability to assess your strengths and weaknesses** – i.e. knowing what you are good and bad at, knowing what tasks are going to be a easy, knowing what tasks are going to be dead hard or beyond you. For example:

   - knowing whether you can do a job you are applying for
   - knowing what you might have to learn in order to apply for a job you want
   - knowing what would be really useful to learn
   - other people knowing that if you say you can do something, you can
   - knowing when not to start something because you can't finish it
   - bettering yourself
   - self-respect
   - being able to be well prepared for anything you can do
   - not boasting about being able to win at pool and losing
   - having the confidence to say if you can do something
   - recognising the skills you do have.

2. **The ability to seek information and advice** – i.e. knowing what to ask, knowing who to ask, sussing things out, checking things out, getting the facts, not being afraid to ask. For example:

   - visiting a business advisory service
   - going to an advice centre to sort out dole/housing problems
   - going to a family planning centre about contraception
   - reading a car repair manual to fix a car
   - going to a college to find out what, courses you can do
   - finding out if you can get a loan from a bank
   - asking if they can make coffee
   - threatening to go to the management committee
   - asking about organising outings
   - finding out where to get new felt for the pool table
   - asking about rights on YTS or ET scheme
   - using a library.

3. **The ability to make decisions** – i.e. making up your mind, getting a real agreement, and sticking to it. For example:

    - deciding whether to go on the enterprise allowance scheme or not
    - deciding where to go on a trip
    - deciding whether to apply for a job or not
    - deciding where to go on an evening
    - deciding how to pick the football team
    - deciding what activities the girls' group is going to do.

4. **The ability to plan time and energy** – i.e. what comes first, what has to be done now and what can be left till later. For example:

    - being efficient at work
    - making the best use of your time
    - getting things done to a deadline
    - organising yourself to carry out a set of tasks, e.g. doctor, shopping, phone call, meals, visits
    - organising your own activities programme
    - planning a meeting.

5. **The ability to carry through agreed responsibilities** – i.e. doing what you said you would do, getting on with things, being dependable. For example:

    - being able to carry out a job given to you by your employer
    - friends can depend on you
    - turning up when you said you would
    - remembering to get the milk
    - finding out something you said you would
    - organising a pool tournament for the junior youth club.

6. **The ability to negotiate** – i.e. wheeling and dealing, striking a bargain, getting the best possible deal. For example:

    - negotiating to buy a motor bike

- getting a landlord to carry out improvements
- negotiating with someone to babysit
- borrowing something from a friend
- deciding where to go on an evening
- persuading staff to keep the club open an extra half hour
- arranging a grant for some equipment.

7. **The ability to deal with people in power and authority** – i.e. 'them' and 'us', people in charge, sorting out the 'big cheeses'. For example:

- dealing with a counter clerk
- trade unionists sorting out problems
- coping with hassle from parents
- coping with hassle from the police
- having power over people at work
- having power over younger brothers and sisters
- arguing with a social worker
- coping with youth workers and community workers
- coping with the police
- dealing with careers or rent officers.

8. **The ability to solve problems** – i.e. sorting things out, overcoming obstacles, finding a solution. For example:

- changing modules on YTS
- coping when you don't get your giro
- paying off debts
- getting repairs done to your house
- sorting out problems with family and friends
- working out how to fix the pool table
- sorting out regulations for child care.

9. **The ability to resolve conflicts** – i.e. not fighting things out, getting over disputes. For example:

- smoking or not smoking in meetings
- resolving a row between friends
- resolving a row in the family
- resolving a row over the pool table
- sorting out arguments over youth club activities.

Resolving a row in the family

10. **The ability to cope with stress and tension** – i.e. not getting really pissed off, being got at, not panicking. For example:

- not worrying your giro won't come and you won't be able to pay off a debt
- not worrying that you might not get the job you have just been interviewed for
- not getting depressed.

...the ability to cope with stress and tension...

11. **The ability to evaluate your own performance** – i.e. knowing how well you did, knowing what went wrong, learning from your mistakes. For example:

- not being like people who say they are good at things and aren't
- not applying for a job you cannot do
- not bragging
- not being over modest
- looking back at things realistically.

12. **The ability to communicate** – i.e. talking to people, letting them know what you think, listening to what others think. For example:

- saying the right thing at a job interview
- explaining you case at the housing office
- not getting in a temper because someone doesn't understand you.

Don't think of these skills as:

- a strict list of skills, the development of which youth workers should adhere to rigorously
- a framework which can be altered, adapted and refined to make them more appropriate to particular circumstances
- a precise definition of terms such as self confidence, social skills, etc.
- everything that youth work is about.

Think of them more as:

- a framework which can be altered, adapted and refined to make them more appropriate to particular circumstances
- a crude breakdown through which we can begin to visualise and put into practice what we hope to achieve
- a useful starting point for this book.

They are also important skills for young people to develop because they:

- are often the sort of skills that are looked for in a job interview
- enable people to cope better with changes in their lives
- enable people to contribute more to their work environment
- enable people to contribute more to their community
- enable people to contribute better to their union
- allow people to make unemployment a more positive experience
- help give people the self-confidence to stand up for themselves
- are needed in a changing world where people need to manage their lives, communities and employment in a creative way.

These core skills also help us begin to understand how youth work can be most effective because they:

- are like sports – you can teach somebody the theory of tennis, or gymnastics, and you can show them role models to impress them, but ultimately, they have to go and practise themselves if they are ever to develop
- help young people recognise that these skills are useful to develop
- help young people see how the skills can be used in different situations

- make it apparent that people already have these skills to some degree or another.

These core skills thus provide part of the framework for this book. Most youth workers will see the value of these skills, the importance of learning by doing or 'experiential learning', and also that it becomes practical to plan and assess programmes and activities. It is almost impossible to plan a session so that 'young people become more able'' but it is possible to plan a session where young people exercise their ability to plan their time and energy, make decisions or negotiate.

This idea of 'learning by doing' or 'experiential education' needs to be looked at quite carefully. If we consider the nature of education and learning, we can identify a number of different ways that people learn.

I. BEING TAUGHT

One way, perhaps the most common in the field of education, is to be taught, to be told, to read, to see, to hear. It is a process through which, knowledge is transferred from one, the teacher, to another, the pupil.

The purpose of such education is usually the acquisition of a certificate and a diploma, and the knowledge that is transferred is usually specified by the curriculum which is controlled by the teacher or the institution they work for. As a result there is, very little opportunity for the learner to have a say in the content of the course or the process by which they are supposed to learn. They are encouraged and directed to do nothing other than absorb the knowledge.

This effectively describes the practice that predominates in most schools, where, for example, the teacher tells the class the dates of the Kings and Queens and, hopefully, the class remembers them. The same happens when we watch television, or read papers and books. It can be a very effective way of learning as the learner can accumulate a lot of information and can remember astonishing quantities of it.

This method of teaching has its place, but, many things that we as youth workers hope young people will learn cannot be 'taught'. You cannot teach someone the difference between right and wrong – it is a personal and individual judgement. You cannot teach someone to have big muscles – they have to develop these themselves. And you cannot teach someone how to create an original work of art – it is something they have to work out or develop for themselves.

In just the same way, it is difficult to teach someone how to 'plan their time and energy' or 'negotiate'. You can teach someone the methods of painting, of body building, of analysing right and wrong, of planning time and energy, or of negotiating, but this does not necessarily mean they can do it for themselves. If we are interested in developing core skills, simply knowing the methods is not good enough; young people will need to exercise them if they are to become more skilled.

2. IMITATION

Another way people learn is from observation and imitation of others. This way of learning can also be very effective; many of us will have imitated pop stars, or trend setters, or adults who have impressed us at some time in our lives, and friends and relatives can be equally influential in our learning. This can also be a powerful way of learning but there is a limit to how much we can control the models young people choose to imitate. We cannot limit the films or television they watch, nor the people they mix with. The main thing we can do is ensure that we, who are often role models for the young people we work with, are good role models and can ensure that the posters, leaflets, videos and so on that we have within the youth project reflect the sort of models that we hope young people will imitate.

3. EXPERIENCE

Another way that people learn is through experience, and this is perhaps the most powerful of all. Learning by mistakes, trying our hand at things, and practice makes perfect are all phrases that suggest the effectiveness of experiential learning, and tests indicate that people remember 20 per cent of what they hear, 40 per cent of what they hear and see, and 80 per cent of what they discover for themselves. If in youth work we hope to develop skills – social skills, life skills, management skills, organisation skills – then we need to recognise that most of these need to be learnt, at least in part, through experience. This makes experiential education a central part of youth work practice and a central part of enabling these sorts of skills to be developed.

Whilst being a central part of youth work practice it is not the only part. It is often beneficial and important to feed in information, to offer ideas, to suggest possible options and to question assumptions that a group may make. Thus 'teaching' has a part to play as well, and part of the art of youth work is to maintain a balance between the two.

There are also clearly times when the risks are too great for young people to experience things for themselves – they might become too disillusioned if it failed, they might suffer physical harm, they might put other people at risk or they might jeopardise the purpose of a project. Youth workers have to balance up these risks and at times will have to restrict the opportunities for experiential learning as a result.

As importantly for these experiences to be most effective, for the lessons learnt to be reinforced, for the skills and knowledge thus gained to be valued and transferred to other situations, the experience needs to be analysed, evaluated, and reflected upon. To exercise a skill and to do nothing is to lose half the effectiveness of that experience. To exercise a skill, and to consider how it went, how effective it was, where else it could be used, what could be done differently next time, is to maximise the educational effect of the experience.

If the development of skills is a central part of youth work, and if these need to be learnt experientially, we also need to appreciate that reflecting upon these experiences is as important as the experience itself. So for the effective development of skills we need to consider how we can get young people to exercise them and to reflect upon their experiences of exercising them. The overall outcome is youth work:

- *young people* being in a position where they have to exercise the core skills for themselves
- *youth workers* planning programmes and activities where young people can exercise core skills.

- *young people* doing things for themselves
- *youth workers* explaining to young people so they understand how they can do things for themselves.

- *young people* being allowed to make mistakes
- *youth workers* ensuring that mistakes are not harmful.

- *young people* considering how effective their actions were
- *youth workers* encouraging this reflection.

- *young people* recognising they have the skills and being able to use them in other circumstances
- *youth workers* helping young people see that the skills are valuable and transferable.

- *young people* exercising skills to a degree that they would not have done otherwise
- *youth workers* ensuring that young people are not frightened off by being asked to do too much.

In practice, the youth worker is trying to develop skills in young people. The possibilities for young people exercising them have to be grabbed. Any given moment can offer the opportunity to get a participant to exercise a skill. Often these opportunities are not very obvious and the youth worker will have to be on the ball to make the most of them.

They will also have a constant awareness of the group and the individuals concerned. The youth worker will need to be considering who may find some tasks onerous, who will find them too easy, who will need support, who needs encouragement and at the same time thinking of appropriate interventions to ensure that these needs may be met.

Underneath all this will be the making of a judgement as things develop between letting young people have a go, making their own mistakes and learning for themselves, on one hand, and the youth worker's legal, professional and ethical responsibilities and the need to protect young people from harm, either physical or mental, on the other. Once again the balance cannot be predicted but can only be described in terms of pushing the young people into exercising skills as far as it is possible but no further. The youth worker is informed by his or her knowledge of the group, the individuals in it, his or her responsibilities and an assessment of what the gains and risks might be.

On top of this, the youth worker will be aware that whenever the skills are exercised the learning can be enhanced if young people are able to reflect upon the experience. Thus there will be times when the youth worker will be thinking of interventions that will enthuse and produce activity, and at others of interventions that calm people down and create a reflective feeling.

This, then, is a general description of what we hope to see in order to enhance skill development with young people. In the second part of this book we will look at how this can be achieved but before that we need to consider what other things we hope to achieve through youth work and consider how these can complement, or contradict, each other.

2 Dialogue

If the development of skills is a central component of good youth work practice, then so, equally, is the developing of coherent values, beliefs and understandings.

There are five things about values, beliefs and understandings that are important to consider if we are to understand how to help develop them.

1. **Values, beliefs and understandings are the things that shape the sort of people we are.** Our characters and lives are largely shaped by the values, beliefs and understandings we hold. They shape the way we relate to other people, the way we organise our lives, the choices we make, the sort of jobs we do, the way we spend our leisure time, the way we conduct our relationships, the sort of friends we have and much, much more. Our values, beliefs and understandings make us the people we are.

2. **Values, beliefs and understandings come from a variety of sources.** They are moulded by everything we experience, the information we receive and the thoughts that we have. They are not fixed, and we know that they change as the information changes, as we encounter new experiences and as we rethink things. The assumptions and standards held by the society around us and the limited information that is available to us shapes our values, beliefs and understandings. The way we are educated, the information we are given, the information we are not given, the laws we are expected to abide by, the things our

parents and friends tell us all go towards the shaping of our values, beliefs and understandings.

The way we collate all this information, the standards by which we judge them, the amount and the way that we think about them and the level of analysis we give them, all lead us towards our own personal set of values (the things we think are important), our particular set of beliefs (the things we think are true about us and the world around us) and understandings (the way we think things work in the world around us). In all probability yours, and mine, are unique for the simple reason that none of us have identical sources of information, identical experiences, identical influences and identical thoughts.

3. **Values, beliefs and understandings are fluid, intertwined and interlinked with each other.** They are 'fluid' because we all have to try to tie together an incredible number of things if we are ever to build up a coherent set of values, beliefs and understandings. We all come across totally conflicting pieces of evidence, a vast array of things that we think are important and a whole range of explanations or understandings of how things work. All these things don't necessarily fit together like a completed jigsaw. Just as we get to the point where we think we know what is most important, we come across something that is more important; just as we arrive at something we believe to be true, we come across something that throws it into doubt; and just as we think we understand how something works, we find an exception. We are all, all the time, trying to tie these things together into a coherent package around which we can organise our life. For all of us this is a constant process as new information, experiences and thoughts keep the whole thing fluid and in constant flux. It is no wonder that, like fingerprints, everyone's outlook, opinions, and particular approach to life are unique.

Many of the things we talk about in youth work, such as 'awareness', 'critical faculties', or 'assertiveness' are about our role in helping people tie their particular set of experiences, information and thoughts together into a more coherent whole, helping them to identify the contradictions, spot the links and find the fallacies.

They are 'intertwined' because the information we come across affects the way we view ourselves and the world around us, while the way we think the world around us works affects the things we think are important, and the things we think are important affect the way we think about things. New information or experiences can change the way we view the world around us, new thoughts can change the things that we think are important and these in turn can change our view of how the world around us works.

They are 'interlinked' because our most cherished values, our most strongly held beliefs and our most well thought out understandings are the end result, the peak, the tip of the iceberg, with a whole range of other values, beliefs and understandings in support.

4. **Values, beliefs and understandings are clung to by people.**
    Youth workers will know that often it can be very difficult to change people's values, beliefs and understandings. There often exists an inbuilt resistance to questioning the values and beliefs they hold. The reasons for this can vary.

One reason might be the fear of being wrong, the fear of losing face, a
fear that everyone holds to some extent or another.

> 'You are never dedicated to something you have complete confidence in. No one is fanatically shouting that the sun is going to rise tomorrow. They know it is going to rise tomorrow. When people are fanatically dedicated to political or religious faiths or any other kind of dogmas or goals, it's always because those dogmas and goals are in doubt.' (Pirsig 1976)

Another reason might be that as we have seen, values, beliefs and understandings are rarely based on any single piece of information or experience. They are often based on a multitude of factors and so it sometimes takes a multitude of other factors to tip the balance and change the value, belief or understanding.

No one is fanatically shouting that the sun is going to rise tomorrow...

A further reason might be that values, beliefs and understandings support each other, are intertwined and interlinked. To change one may involve changing a whole number of others. Changing values and beliefs can lead to an upheaval in your life that is often easier to avoid altogether. It is easy to see why conventional wisdom resists such change so stoutly:

> 'It is far, far easier to have a firm anchor in nonsense than to put out in the troubled seas of thought.' (Galbraith 1977)

5. **Values, beliefs and understandings are not facts.** Facts and truths are things that we know, things that are not in doubt, things that can be proven, and they are few and far between. Even in the purest of sciences it is now recognised that knowledge is far from certain. Few things are any longer 100 per cent, indisputable truths. Things that were taken as facts, as absolute truths such as time or space or a flat earth have all been

brought into question. No longer are they necessarily true, no longer are they absolute facts, but relative, wrong or ill-defined.

> '...there is no absolute knowledge. And those who claim it, whether they are scientists or dogmatists, open the door to tragedy. All information is imperfect. We have to treat it with humility.' (Bronowski 1973)

If science which has always had an aura of truth, factuality and proof about it now has to question its most basic assumptions, then where does that leave us with our values, beliefs and understandings?

What all these features of values, beliefs and understandings help us to understand is that helping young people build a coherent package is fundamental to achieving things such as 'awareness', 'sensitivity', 'empowerment' and so on. We can also see that if we are to be effective in helping young people sort them out we need a method that does not simply offer one explanation of why they might need to change them, one experience, one piece of information, one of our thoughts, because values, beliefs and understandings are complex and intertwined and change comes by degrees, not all at once. We have to offer as many pieces of information, as many experiences and as many opportunities for thinking about it as possible. All these gradually tip the balance, sway opinion, and shift the sands.

> 'Let us now sum up something of the nature of argument. To convince someone of something we work back to beliefs he/she already holds and argue from them as premises. Perhaps we also insinuate some supporting beliefs, as needed further premises. We may succeed in insinuating a further belief simply by stating it, or we may be called upon to offer further support for it in turn. We aim, of course, for supporting beliefs that the person is readier to adopt than the thing we are finally trying to convince him/her of. His/her readiness to adopt what we put to him/her will depend partly on its intrinsic plausibility and partly on his/her confidence in us.' (Quine and Ullian 1978)

We need a method that does not simply question the things that come out in normal conversation, because to just question or challenge is not likely to be very successful. Unless you have exceptional sway with an individual, exceptional trust and exceptional respect, one question or one challenge is unlikely to change their views. In most instances, change only comes about when we begin to look under the surface, go beyond the superficial and begin to consider the underlying reasons for such values, beliefs and understandings. Challenging these superficial things also carries with it the risk that young people might simply say what they think you want to hear. This is a hollow achievement since values, beliefs and understandings have not changed at all and the opportunities to look at the underlying values, beliefs and under-standings may well be restricted as a result.

We need a method that does not assume that we know what particular experiences, what specific pieces of information, what pat-terns of thought may have led an individual to a particular value, belief or understanding. We need to be able to explore these, to shift as the thought patterns become clear, as the particular experiences are revealed and as the specific pieces of information are unveiled. We need to be able to move at tangents, to be able to hop from issue to issue, from fact to fact and from thought to thought. We need to be able to follow any emerging thread and we must not be restricted to specific topics or areas of knowledge.

We need a method that does not encourage people to cling to their values, beliefs and understandings, because nothing will otherwise really change. In the first place this means building up a maximum level of trust, support and respect. The more trust, the less the fear of being wrong; the more respect, the less people will feel exposed; and the more support, the more people will feel able to rearrange their values, beliefs and understandings, even if this leads to upheaval.

'The wise man says "I am looking for the truth", the fool says "I have found the truth".' (Russian proverb)

'One of the greatest pieces of wisdom is to know what you do not know.' (Galbraith 1977)

So if we want people to think about and change their values, beliefs and understandings we have to:

- Offer as many pieces of information, as many experiences and as many opportunities for thinking about them as possible.

- Begin to look under the surface, go beyond the superficial and begin to consider the underlying reasons for such values, beliefs and understandings.
- Explore these, to shift as the thought patterns become clear, as the particular experiences are revealed and as the specific pieces of information are unveiled.
- Build up a maximum level of trust, support and respect.

This is called 'dialogue' – a process where we try to create situations where both the young person and the youth worker are able to explore and question the underlying values, beliefs and understandings, find fallacies, discover irrational and inconsistent conclusions and rebuild consistent, rational and realistic values, beliefs and understandings in their place.

Dialogue is not	Dialogue is
something alien, complicated, nor abstract	something that most youth workers use in their work
just chatting, which tends to be about daily events and about 'what' is happening around us	those times when we get a group to think about and discuss things that are not simply superficial, but underlie the day-to-day events, not what is happening around us but why these things are happening around us
arguing or debating, which tends to be competitive, and tends to have a winner or a loser.	a shared exploration, an investigation in which participants go deeper than simple conversation, and consider questions rather than answer them.

'The desire to be right and the desire to have been right are two separate desires, to be right is the thirst for truth, to have been right is the pride that goeth before the fall. It stands in the way of our seeing we are wrong, and thus blocks the progress of our knowledge. It plays hell with our credibility rating.' (Quine and Ullian 1978)

...the desire to be right or the desire to have been right...

Dialogue is not	Dialogue is
a discussion group, nor informal, nor social education	a specific activity, which can be identified, and often comes out of chatting, or as part of discussion groups and is part of informal or social education
restricted to specific preordained areas of exploration	something that moves at tangents and is applicable to any question, any issue, even if there are not right and wrong answers, in fact especially where there are dilemmas to be considered and where values, beliefs and understandings are part of the equation

a competitive, win or lose process.	an exchange of feelings, an exchange of thoughts, an exchange of information and an exchange of understandings.

'Tolerance, comes in three forms, one is to tolerate other views but not really care about them, the other is to tolerate views because there may be some truth in it. One is respectful, the other is not... The third type is tolerance to the point that I might have to change my life as my values and beliefs change. Hold one's opinions as long as one honestly believe they have better rational support than others, but also being able to relinquish them when one's reasons for holding them cease to be compelling.' (Lipman 1988)

Dialogue is not

something that happens at the snap of your fingers, something concrete, that either is or is not happening.

Dialogue is

something that drifts from chat, to discussion, to dialogue, and drifts back the other way.

'...students began by talking about everyday issues, and ended up talking about hard core philosophical issues.' (Lipman 1988)

'One cannot help thinking of the analogy of walking, where you move forward by constantly throwing yourself off balance. When you walk, you never have both feet solidly on the ground at the same time. Each step forward makes a further step forward possible; in a dialogue, each argument evokes a counterargument that pushes itself beyond the other and pushes the other beyond itself.' (Lipman 1991)

Dialogue is not

a vague idea that is impossible to do in practice

Dialogue is

something that does have an impact on young people and something that we feel good about when it happens a way for values, beliefs and understandings to be taught. another form of experiential education. Participants experience the dilemmas, the contradictions, the flaws and experience the resolving of them.

'The teacher is no longer the exclusive educator in the group but becomes together with everyone else in the group, a co-investigator of reality.' (Allman, in O'Hagan 1991)

Most youth workers, if they think about times when they feel they have made some contribution to young people developing a coherent package of values, beliefs and understandings will, on reflection, recognise that this process, 'the building of dialogue', will have taken place. It may have happened whilst sitting round a camp fire drinking hot chocolate; it may have happened in the back of a minibus on the way back from an away football match; or it may have happened in a user committee meeting. It may have happened whilst sitting in the office late in the evening; it may have happened sitting on a wall outside the betting shop; or it may have happened after watching a video.

...dialogue building can happen in almost any circumstances...

Dialogue building can happen in almost any circumstances. It may have lasted for two minutes or it may have lasted for an hour. It may have been about drugs, or relationships, or aggression, or it may have been about being a woman, or disabled, or black. Dialogue can happen at almost any time and it can be about almost anything. It can be triggered off by an infinite amount of things, planned or unplanned, but, whatever the circumstances we, as youth workers, usually recognise it as valuable to our work. When it happens we feel that we have achieved something, and people really thought about and shared something, we feel that we got somewhere, and we feel that it had an effect on the participants. Often when it happens, when we have a really good session where issues are considered in some depth, with real concern and thought, we come away from it walking on air and can't wait to relate the incident to our colleagues.

So far we have looked at the development of skills and values, beliefs and understandings, and we have been able to see a little clearer what these terms mean, and how this development might come about. In both these dialogue had a key part to play and the same can be said for our third set of objectives in youth work – the development of autonomous, thinking, assertive and critical faculties in young people.

A slightly different field of education that has also developed the use of dialogue is a schools programme in America called 'Philosophy for Children', originated by Mathew Lipman. He was a teacher of philosophy and used dialogue as a method of encouraging classes of children, as young as five years old, to consider philosophical issues. Having developed this programme, he became convinced that it was doing far more than simply teaching philosophical issues; he felt that it was doing nothing less than teaching children how to think. He argues that traditional methods in schools teach children facts, fill them full of hard information, but do little to enable them to think for themselves. Dialogue is dependent on the participants thinking for themselves. By its nature it does not offer clear answers but stimulates individuals to consider their thoughts on the subject and enables those thoughts to be questioned and analysed. The 'Philosophy for Children' programme lays claim to some staggering results. One programme in New Jersey advanced the children's mental age by 27 months in the space of nine weeks; another, with a difficult class coming up to school leaving age, resulted in 100 per cent of the class deciding that they would stay on at school to study further. Whilst results like this may not be replicated everywhere, it is an indication that using dialogue is an education in itself, building awareness, confidence and the ability to think independently.

Paulo Freire was a teacher of literacy from Brazil. He found that he could use literacy as a vehicle for building dialogue. This dialogue led to an increase in the political awareness of the peasants he worked with. By building a dialogue that was relevant to the peasants' life, he found that they learnt how to read and write much quicker and developed a much stronger consciousness of what was wrong with their community and society, and what to do about it. He called this process 'conscientization'. When Brazil suffered a military coup he was imprisoned and later expelled from the country. He continued to write and talk about his view of education and continues to be a major influence on much of the liberation theology, development practice and educational theory in the undeveloped world (Freire 1970, 1976).

Many people who have come across this style of work have thought that it is only applicable to third world countries where the problems are so much more apparent and immediate. In reality most of the tasks that groups take on are as mundane as those that community groups might do in the first world. They are more likely to be working on a way to keep the pigs off the vegetables than they are to be changing the caste system, and they are more likely to be building a water cart than campaigning against the river authorities. Paulo Freire used literacy as the vehicle through which he could facilitate a critical awareness and the projects that your group come up with are likely to be no more spectacular in themselves, but nevertheless they allow the opportunity for the process to be equally productive.

The process of dialogue helps young people to sort out their own coherent set of beliefs, their own values, the result of which is greater self-esteem, a greater level of self-confidence, and a greater awareness of the issues around them and their complexities. Dialogue helps young people question what they see, hear and are told, it builds critical faculties, it exposes them to other views and opinions, and helps them to appreciate that many issues are not right or wrong but genuine moral dilemmas. It builds the capacity to make moral judgements with care and thought, and it helps people to become critical participants in life, rather than prejudiced subjects of life.

In terms of dialogue we are thus looking for a situation where:

- *young people* are able to explore their values, beliefs and understandings
- *youth workers* create circumstances where this is valued and encouraged.

- *young people* look under the surface of their values, beliefs and understandings
- *youth workers* offer information, experiences and facilitation to enable this to happen.

- *young people* have the freedom to explore their values, beliefs and understandings in any direction
- *youth workers* are sensitive to the varying strands of thought that might emerge but may guide the discussion in a particular direction at times.

- *young people* do not feel they have to cling to their values, beliefs and understandings
- *youth workers* build up a maximum level of trust and respect to help young people feel comfortable about taking risks.

- *young people's and youth workers'* values, beliefs and understandings are treated with respect, but equally are open to question
- *young people and youth workers* contribute towards a shared exploration, an investigation, a 'community of enquiry'.

'The teacher's role is not that of a supplier of values, but on of facilitating and clarifying the valuing process.' (Lipman 1988)

What does dialogue building look like in practice? This process is eloquently explained in this excerpt about the 'Philosophy for Children' programme.

'While listening is important for the children, for the teacher it is fundamental to the success of achieving genuine discussion. It is only by the most careful listening that the teacher will become aware of the range of opinions on a given topic, and be able to devise questions to promote dialogue between protagonists. Then there will be a need to consider which exercises from the manual would be useful for illuminating some idea that the children have raised; the need to remember fleeting contributions for future use, particularly if they raise further issues that need to be considered; noticing when the discussion has become sidetracked from the original question, deciding to what extent the side-track is worthwhile, and when the moment might be opportune for returning to the main topic. The prime motivation for these decisions is always what will maintain the children's interest and involvement...there is more. It is the teacher's job to notice mistakes in reasoning that are overlooked by the group, and devise ways of drawing attention to them; to insist that those doing the most talking are also prepared to listen, and to make sure that those who prefer to talk less have the opportunity to express themselves when they wish.

"Wisdom is decided into two parts, (1) having a great deal to say, (2) not saying it." (Anon)

One measure of success will be the amount of talking the teacher has to do, which should be as little as possible. The more controversial and problematic the topic, the more likely it is to engage the children's interest, to the extent that they will often initiate dialogue between themselves; and when this happens the teacher can and should revert purely to listening, coming in with further questions only when the children themselves seem to have reached an impasse.' (Whalley, in Coles and Robinson 1989)

3 Groups

Having considered the development of skills, values, beliefs and under-standings and critical, autonomous and assertive faculties, we now need to look at one particular way we work with young people – in groups.

> 'group (-oo-). 1. n Number of persons or things near together, or belonging or classed together; (Art) two or more figures &c. forming a complete design or distinct part of one; g.-captain, a R.A.F. OFFICER. 2. v.t. & i. Form, fall, into a g.;place in a g. (with, together); form (colours, figures, &c.) into a harmonious whole; classify. [It.]' (Concise Oxford Dictionary)

Groups are the basic building block of society. It is through groups that society has historically accomplished tasks such as childcare, hunting, music, and protest; provided support and affection through families, tribes and clans; and created and passed on culture, knowledge, mean-ings, politics and language.

For nearly all youth workers, working with groups makes for a substantial part of their face-to-face work. There are a number of reasons for this, some obvious, for example, they are more economic, as few youth projects can justify working on a one-to-one basis all of the time. Others are not so obvious.

- Many of the things we hope young people will gain from youth work are to do with an individual's ability to relate to others, e.g. to cooperate, to develop stable relationships, to work as part of a team – all things that inevitably are better done in a group context where such issues arise.

...society has historically...

- Dialogue is best built within a group context where there is a breadth of input, thought, information and opinions.
- People, by nature, like company and respond to demands, encouragement and criticism from other group members.
- People respond to group pressure because they fear being rejected by the group.
- People respond to group pressure because they want to feel wanted by the group.
- People identify their needs with those of the group, i.e. they all share a common aim.
- Groups can produce results that would not normally be produced by individuals. Just think of a project which you have seen carried out by a group and think how improbable it is that an individual in that group would have done it on his or her own.
- Groups can develop a momentum of their own which can carry individuals through problems and over difficulties that would normally bring them to a halt.

- A group can generate its own energy to do this and brings together a wide variety of thoughts, skills and talents that are available for all members to see, use and learn.
- Groups also tend to develop a personality, style and nature of their own.
- A group is a natural way for people to work. From villages to families and from clubs to work, people operate in groups.

So you are not trying to force something unnatural on people. However, many young people have experienced an education system that does not encourage people to work and learn together so there is a need for some reeducation or de-schooling to help people regain their natural ability.

Groups are so much at the centre of our lives and our work as youth workers that it is easy to take them for granted, although over the last hundred years the traditional groups that people belonged to such as the church and the extended family have been in part replaced by other groups such as encounter groups, interest groups, cause groups, pressure groups, cultural groups and community groups.

Over the years groups have been studied by psychologists, sociologists, social psychologists, psychiatrists, psychoanalysts, anthropologists, management theorists, social workers and educationalists. Whilst there has not been unanimous agreement between all these schools, there is some consensus that there are a number of key factors that affect the way that groups work:

1. **Relationships** – in a group of eight members there are 28 different relationships at work; as any one of these change so it may influence others. In any group we work with we can see this at work; changing alliances, friendships, jealousy, competition and many other factors all affect and are affected by the changing relationships. Thus the state of the relationships within a group can be a major factor in the way it operates. For example, a group with a high degree of competition and little affection between members will be different from a group with a high degree of cooperation and a great deal of affection. So relationships between members of the group, particularly regarding gender, race, age, class, power and ability, have an influence on the way a group works. Relationships are tricky and

unpredictable things and in any group the relationships between the individuals are always in a constant state in flux.

2. **Aims** – fundamental to holding the group together and providing the motivation for individuals to take part. This is not simply about the central aim of a group, which provides the bond, but also about the secondary aims. In many groups individuals may be part of them to achieve the primary aim, but also secondary aims. These may range from wanting a good laugh to making money, and from making a new friend to not being bored. A successful group is one that manages to combine all these aims successfully.

3. **Norms** – the expectations of behaviour, the ground rules adopted by a group, often not even written or spoken rules. It is easy to see the difference between a group where the norms are violent and uncaring, and one where violence is abhorred and caring about other members is valued. The setting of norms is often fixed by the circumstances under which groups meet, but usually near the beginning of the groups' formation. Once set they can be very hard to change because they are part and parcel of the culture of the group.

4. **Decisions** – often considered to be the central function of a group, and consequently the way they are made can be very illuminating on the participatory state of the group. Decisions lead to the setting of short- and long-term aims and we have already seen how important they are in terms of forming and motivating a group. As a result, the more participative a decision, the stronger the commitment is likely to be and the stronger the group.

5. **Roles** – people finding a role they are comfortable with and recognising other people's roles. This does not mean things like chairperson, secretary or treasurer, although these may be useful roles. People can perform all sorts of useful roles in a group ranging from the one who makes everyone else laugh, the one who looks after the underdog, the one who is critical, the one who initiates discussion, the one who clarifies discussions, and so on. The roles that people adopt can be a challenge to them,

but it can also be a way of finding a safe corner that does not place any responsibilities or expectations upon them.

6. **Communication** – how it is organised and by whom. Participatory decisions, stable and mature relationships, changed norms, and clear aims all depend on effective communication within a group. Communication is partly about individual abilities such as who has the loudest voice, who has the information, how articulate an individual is and how good people are at listening, and partly about the vocabulary that is used and the time available for it.

There is also some consensus about the phases that groups go through. This is outlined below:

1. All are individuals and have not yet begun to form into a group.

2. People begin to discover common areas of interest and start to make tentative relationships; leaders begin to emerge and norms begin to be established.

3. Relationships strengthen, cliques begin to develop, norms are strengthened, individuals' roles become clearer. This phase is often seen as a honeymoon period.

4. Leadership roles are clarified; continued strengthening of roles, norms and goals occurs.

5. The cohesion of the group grows and the influence of the group on the individual increases.

6. Patterns of the group are well established, and a good deal of stability exists.

7. Goals have been attained, there is no longer a common aim, and instability may follow.

This is not a prescription of the way groups have to develop but a description of the way they often do. One thing that is clear is that the more time people have in the earlier stages, the more chance of finding a cohesiveness and balance later on. As with much else in youth work, slow but sure development will produce the best results in the long run.

There are a number of other things that we need to consider about working with groups in the context of youth work. We have seen how the aim is the thing that makes a number of individuals into a group. It is the magnet that draws them together, the purpose for being there and the glue that provides the bond. It is also the key factor in motivating the members of the group.

Motivation is the link between ideas and action. It isn't possible to be motivated without an idea to direct it. Motivation describes the action of putting an idea into practice. This means that to be motivated, the idea has to 'grab' an individual, it has to appeal to them, but it also has to be achievable for them to pursue it. Such is human nature that it is almost impossible to predict what will 'grab' who and as a result youth workers need to be broad-minded about the sort of aims a group might set itself. The possibilities of achieving it are more within the control of the youth worker, although often young people may take some convincing.

...motivation...

So having an aim in itself is not enough to hold a group together; it also has to be an aim that motivates. This, however, applies more to some groups than others. The sort of groups we work with tend to vary. At one extreme we work with groups that are made up of close friends, often a gang, or a girls' group. These groups have usually already formed before we start working with them. As a result, they have already gone through the process outlined above. The individuals have found their roles, leaders have emerged, norms have been set and relationships are well developed. When we are working with groups such as these, often called 'primary' groups, the aim becomes less important. The bond between the members, the magnet that pulls them together, is not the achievement of specific goals, although it might be this as well; it is the bond of affection and the emotional ties between the members. This may have advantages in some ways but in others it has distinct disadvantages. Skills are less likely to be exercised if the group has no specific aims other than to be together but sitting round and chatting is very conducive to building dialogue. Primary groups also exercise a high degree of influence over their members, they play a powerful part in the shaping of our values, beliefs and understandings, and consequently can play a powerful part in us changing them. However, they are difficult to create, they usually grow organically, out of our control or influence, somewhat unpredictably and often over long periods of time.

Primary groups tend to have particular characteristics. For example, the group takes little work to keep it together, and relationships are more developed, norms set, and roles adopted. Members are quite happy to sit and chat about things with little encouragement, but they are not so likely to exercise skills, they can be difficult to change if they are not conducive to skills development or dialogue, and members are less likely to question each other's opinions.

> 'The first assumption to be made is that the gang is a group, in the sense that there is a pattern of relationships and a common aim either in existence or at least potentially there, something which can be made use of.' (Kuenstler 1960)

At the other extreme we have 'secondary' groups. These are groups that may never have met before as a group and as a result have yet to work through the process of forming relationships, setting norms, selecting leaders and so on. For these groups specified aims become much more important; without one that appeals to them all the group is unlikely to stay together. Secondary groups are usually less consensual than their primary counterparts. In primary groups the developed relationships, the accepted norms and the adopted roles all contribute towards a group that tends to agree, to go along and to cover for each other. This is a very comfortable position for all concerned but can mean that it is less productive in youth work terms. The conflicts that arise around relationships, norms and aims can be very productive in terms of dialogue building and these crop up with more regularity in a secondary group than a primary one.

Secondary groups also tend to have particular characteristics. For example, the group has to go through all the difficulties of establishing relationships, setting norms and adopting roles, trust has to be built up, and a clear aim is of central importance. However, it creates opportunities for dialogue and youth workers have greater influence over the norms, relationships and roles, members are more likely to be responsive to criticism, and individuals are more likely to exercise skills.

Groups, of course, can fit anywhere between these two extremes and over time groups often progress from one to the other. But whatever sort they are, it affects the way we work with them. Overall, we can see that for our purposes we need to work towards developing particular group characteristics. For example:

- Relationships are such that people feel part of a group, there is respect between the members and there is a high degree of trust.

- Norms are such that everyone is accountable, discussion is acceptable, actions are justifiable, individuals take responsibility, all members are entitled to equal participation and they are clear.

- Aims are such that they appeal to all members, are agreed upon, and are clear.

- Roles are such that people feel comfortable in them, they are challenged by them, they are valued, and the youth worker's role is understood.

- Decisions are such that everyone has a say in them and they are not divisive.

- Communication is such that it is open and respectful, everyone can participate, and people listen as well as speak.

...the youth worker's role is understood...

This all means that groups usually need to have between five and fifteen members.

In practice, the youth worker has to consider a myriad of different factors. On one point he or she is clear: the group should be as much like our ideal, outlined earlier, as possible. But this ideal has to be applied in practice. The youth worker has to be constantly aware of how the group is working. Are people antagonistic to each other? Are people able to be honest? Do people feel valued? Is everyone happy with decisions? And how motivated are they? Balanced against this is the knowledge that young people are here out of choice, they need to get what they want out of it and the more it is their group and the more it is their aims, the greater their commitment and achievement will be.

Every second of every session the worker may hold with the group, these sorts of things have to be balanced against each other. When to intervene is not a straightforward question and the only answer is as much as is possible at any given moment. The more a group can be shaped to the ideal, the better it will be in terms of educational outcomes, but to push too hard can result in a deterioration of trust, ownership and commitment.

The result is a constantly changing level of intervention; some moments a group may be allowed a free rein, whilst others the youth worker may apply considerable pressure. The information to make these momentary decisions is gleaned from young people's comments, the attendance, the enthusiasm or lack of it in people's voices or actions, the progress, the looks on young people's faces, the body language and a hundred other minuscule factors that we may notice.

The youth worker is thus in a position of receiving vast quantities of information, of evaluating this on the spot, and of constructing responses that are appropriate to the development of the group but maintain the young people's feeling of ownership. The difficulties in doing this are complicated by the fact that the group is constantly changing as relationships change, as external factors affect it, as it progresses through different stages and as and when the membership changes. What may have been a perfect intervention the previous week may turn out to be the worst possible this week.

We have now looked at what a youth worker is trying to achieve – for example, building dialogue, developing skills, and developing appropriate groups. What we are looking at is a youth worker with a particular style and a particular role in relation to the young people they are working with. For example, to develop the skills, it requires a youth worker who can enable young people to learn experientially and is able to intervene when necessary to encourage young people and protect them from any harm. To build dialogue, we need youth workers to encourage young people to explore their thoughts in an atmosphere of trust and respect. And to develop appropriate groups, we need youth workers who can allow the group to develop in such a way that the participants feel it is their group, but they also have to ensure that the nature of the group does not undermine the youth work itself.

Youth workers need to tailor these three objectives together into a harmonious whole. This is not as difficult as it may seem in that in all three objectives the youth worker is trying to pass over to the young people opportunities for them to take some control, and in all three objectives there are commonalities of action and reflection.

The hallmarks of this role or style is the thoughtful and respectful exercise of power, the development of trust, and evaluation, and these are worth looking at in a little more detail along with some consideration of the context in which youth workers operate.

4 Power and Trust

Power lies at the core of the question of intervention – 'To intervene or not to intervene? That is the question.' And interventions in effect mean the exercise of power.

In the preceding sections we have looked at how youth workers have to strike a balance between allowing young people to exercise skills and learn through their mistakes, and not letting them make such big mistakes that they get into difficulties; pushing groups into building dialogue, and letting it develop on their own terms; and shaping groups to suit our purposes, and allowing young people to shape their own groups. All these are about when and when not to exercise power.

There are different reasons why youth workers have power and influence over a group. These include:

- **Their position**, which gives them rights and powers and authority. This, probably the most obvious source of power, comes from the authority that is vested in a youth worker and is usually seen in the context of rules, regulations and responsibilities.

- **Their expertise and knowledge**, which is likely to be greater in most areas. Their sources of information are likely to be more extensive, their experience is likely to be greater, their ability to persuade is likely to be more developed and their ability to deceive will be much more accomplished.

- **Their individual standing and respect**, which allows youth workers to exert influence through the respect held for them, the example they set and the wish on the part of young people to be approved.

- **Their control over resources.** An obvious form of power is that of coercion or induction, or bribes and sanctions: again one that is apparent in all our lives and is used extensively by youth workers in allocating or not allocating access to funds, time and equipment.

- **Their control over the context in which youth work is carried out.** One way to exercise power is through manipulation of the environment. This in crude terms can mean keeping certain doors locked in a youth project or restricting access for certain young people, and power in this form is regularly seen in youth projects. It can also operate on a more subtle level, in that sometimes young people can be convinced of the restrictions in their environment without having to actually see them. For example, a group may be told there is no money in the budget, without them actually seeing or understanding the books. Their behaviour or demands will be changed accordingly. Another example would be the expectations in general that young women are only interested in sewing, children or cooking. If this view pervades the environment, it is likely that it will restrict young women in their choices of activity.

If young people are to feel part of a group they need to be able to participate in the shaping of it; if young people are to exercise skills they need to be able to participate in the action; and if young people are to participate in dialogue, they need to participate in the direction it takes and the subject it covers. For any of this to happen youth workers have to temper their near monopoly of power.

This is not always easy to achieve. On one hand we need to temper our power so that, for example, young people:

- take the maximum responsibility
- feel committed to the aims of a group
- have to exercise skills
- are able to explore their own values, beliefs and understandings
- feel able to question youth workers' values, beliefs and understandings
- are able to make mistakes
- are able to contribute towards a dialogue and have their opinions respected.

However, this cannot mean an abdication of all responsibility for what happens. Youth workers have responsibilities as well and the art of youth work is achieving the best possible balance between this need to temper their power and the need to exercise it. We have to exercise power so that, for example:

- young people do not come to harm
- young people do not destroy trust in a group
- young people's values, beliefs and understandings are questioned
- young people do not break the law
- mistakes are not damaging
- young people exercise skills
- relationships do not destroy a group
- norms do not prevent skill development and dialogue
- communication is not restricted
- aims are achievable
- everyone is able to participate.

...young people do not come to harm...

In terms of ensuring that events and circumstances do not prevent the practice of good youth work or lead to young people coming to harm, we use it a lot more forcefully. Theft, vandalism, aggression, offensive behaviour, poor health and safety and bullying would damage proceedings. In these events we may well use all the power at our disposal in order to ensure that these things do not happen and that it is possible to practise good youth work. In these circumstances, the exercise of power may well be open to criticism and questioning, but ultimately it is not open to rejection. It is thus an unnegotiable exercise of power.

In other circumstances we may be willing to negotiate our exercise of power; not only will it be questionable and open to criticism, but its use will also be open to rejection. Our offer to make decisions, to plan activities, or to choose who joins a group may be resisted and may be allowed to be resisted. Pushing at the frontiers of control is inevitable and we, as youth workers, need to be able to recognise that this is happening, not take it personally and be clear as to how far we are prepared to allow the frontiers to be moved.

The exercise of power need not be problematic in terms of the method. If youth workers are honest about it, if they care to explain the reasons why they might not be prepared to negotiate and if they are open to questioning and criticism, the exercise of power is less likely to prove difficult and in fact can be a productive vehicle upon which dialogue can be built.

In this instance, the youth worker has to be constantly pushing the agenda, the discussion, the actions and the development of the group as far as possible in a direction that leads to the best results. This may be achieved through a whole range of ways. They may try persuasion, or shouting, they may make deals, they may offer inducements. It could involve careful arrangements for meetings and it may involve some sort of sanctions, even if this is only the disapproval of the youth worker. However, whilst the youth worker wants to push things as far as possible, there are limits. Push too hard and young people will stop attending; push too quickly and young people will not feel it is their group; push too far and young people will lose the commitment that comes about as a result of their ownership of the aim; and push too quickly in discussions about personal matters and young people will stop thinking about them.

The decision of how far to push is momentary and often a guess. The decision about how hard to push and when will be made on the basis of the youth worker's knowledge of the young people, the looks on their faces, the tone of their voices, the way they sit and a hundred other things. They will know, from previous consideration, at which point their exercise of power becomes nonnegotiable. When it is, they will have to construct appropriate interventions on the spot, although they may well have built up a repertoire over time. Each will have to be finely tailored to the individual or group concerned and this will have to be done instantly. The interventions will need to be appropriate to the circumstances but will also have to be flexible.

In other circumstances they will be prepared to be more flexible. If their use of power does not seem to be getting the desired response they might have to change it, withdraw it or play it down. They are consequently involved in a constant process of negotiation, giving on some things, pushing on others, and allowing the young people to push back and respond on their side.

Throughout the practice of youth work, negotiation is the prevailing tendency and the youth worker's exercise of power has to be, where ever possible, in the same vein.

This then is not an abdication of power but a respectful and considered exercise, and what is important is that this exercising is done in such a way that it has a minimal impact upon the participation we want to encourage, but protects the individual and the process from harm.

Power is not something that can be given away but it is something that can be held back. One of the hardest things about this style of youth work is not exercising power. This is the only way that young people are going to have the opportunity to exercise it for themselves. It is through our thoughtful and respectful exercise of power that we enable young people to develop skills, look at their understandings, values and beliefs, and participate in the formation of groups.

To this understanding we need to add the need for trust. We have seen that trust is a prerequisite for effective dialogue building. We have already looked at a number of reasons why people are less likely to explore and consider their values, beliefs and understandings. For instance, they might feel they:

• are going to get mocked

- are going to be rejected
- are going to lose face
- are going to be wrong
- will not be supported
- are not respected.

...they feel they are going to lose face...

Trust is also important if young people are able to learn other things, such as exercising skills, the ability to take chances with tasks that they might find challenging, and the ability to be open about such things as their strengths and weaknesses, stress and tension and evaluating their own performance.

There are also good reasons why trust is important for the development of groups; it helps with dealing with their dynamics honestly, discussing power openly, and feeling able to commit themselves to the group.

For all these sorts of reasons the development of trust is an important part of good youth work.

Trust is the feeling that another will not fail them, a feeling that there is no need for defensiveness, and it is built over time, in small ways, through little tests. Tones of voice are listened to, actions are watched, and gradually trust will grow. As it grows, so the building of dialogue will be able to grow. A group without trust will have conversations that are stilted, cautious and superficial. The depth of trust bears a direct relationship to the depth of dialogue.

The size of the group you work with will have a direct relationship to this. The more people there are, the more likely it is that an individual will find someone in whom they do not feel able to place their trust. It is obvious that on a one-to-one basis trust will grow much quicker. Often large groups breaking into little ones will allow a greater openness on the part of the participants. This fact has to be balanced against the advantages to the building of dialogue in having larger groups with a wider range of views, opinions, experiences and ideas.

A youth worker building trust knows that the growth of trust is a difficult thing to determine. It has its own way of developing, but, more than anything else, the youth worker knows that it grows through little things and he or she will consequently be aware of his or her tone of voice, actions, body language and so on. They will also know that it has to be genuine; a pretence at being trustworthy is unlikely to succeed and a young person's trust only has to be failed once and the rebuilding can be near to impossible. The youth worker will be operating with this in mind all the time.

They will take care to promise no more than they can deliver and will make sure that they respect confidentialities and offer support, advice and encouragement whenever necessary. They will want young people to be able to express their views and opinions and they will not betray the trust the young person has in them, nor mock or belittle them when contentious views are expressed. They will be trying to create a norm of trust and as a result they will be open and trusting, and willing to be as trusting of the young people as they expect them to be of each other and of him- or herself.

5 Evaluation

It will be clear to anyone reading this book that style and role for a youth worker are neither easy or simple. The plans, actions and responses of youth workers are based on judgements, not concrete facts and plans. They will be based on the skills, knowledge and personality of the particular youth worker, and they will be adapted to suit the particular group.

This does not mean that it is impossible – far from it – but it does mean that each youth worker has to develop their own style of delivering their own methods in their particular circumstances. Consequently, they need to think about evaluation and above all this means a reflective practice. We are not working with fixed, unchanging, predictable circumstances and we have to continually exercise our judgement, make decisions on the spot, make interventions and deal with different reactions to them. All this requires constant reflection upon our practice.

Our experience formed the basis of this book, but as with all youth workers, much of that experience is the result of guess work, intuition, gut feeling and instinct. These terms describe an instant conclusion, a conclusion that we don't arrive at through a conscious process of deduction or elimination, but one that we arrive at through a whole variety of bits of knowledge and experience that automatically directs our thoughts towards a conclusion. It is because we are not aware of them as a conscious process of thought that we call them hunches, intuition, gut feelings or instincts.

For example, most youth workers will have experienced incidents where two young people are getting edgy with each other. All of us, when we see it happening, will try to gauge what to do. Is it all bravado? Perhaps it is best left to sort itself out. Is it going to get heavy? Perhaps it is best that we do something to stop it. If we need to do something to stop it, what would be the best thing to do? How can we avoid physical violence, a bloody nose for the youth worker, our authority being undermined, our relationship with one protagonist being damaged, and so on?

These thoughts go through our mind so quickly that we are not even aware of them as questions. On top of this we also usually come up with an answer, what we would describe as a hunch, and upon this we act. The arrival at an answer is even more astonishing in its speed than setting the question. From a whole variety of sources ranging from the body language of the two individuals involved, to the tone of their voice, from the circumstances in which the conflict has arisen, to the way people around the two protagonists are behaving; these multitude of factors shape the answer that we come up with.

If we decide that we do need to intervene we then have to decide how. Once again there may be a whole list of factors that affect this decision: past experience, our knowledge of the individuals involved, our experience of what has worked before and what has not, what resources we have, and many other factors. All this information is assimilated without our even being aware of it and our intervention is then carried out.

This whole process, from the moment we see it to the moment we act, may only take a few seconds, but in that space of time dozens of factors may have been processed through our brain and a conclusion reached. For such a complex and astonishing ability we use the word hunch, or gut feeling, or intuition, none of which really do it justice.

There is nothing wrong with hunches, intuition and gut feelings in youth work but they are not enough, and once again we have to find a balance. To not operate on hunches, gut feelings and intuition is not only impossible but also impractical. Apart from the fact that every incident that happened would see us disappearing off into the office to work out what to do, it would also make us unhuman. To take away all spontaneity, all emotion, all risk, all error and all spirit would be to make us into automatons – unfeeling, cold and predictable machines. As youth workers we need to be able to move with the flow, be surprised, be wrong, be funny, and so on. We need to be human. So hunches are okay and are only a reflection of the fact that we are real people and not machines. Becoming too conscious of our actions, becoming too cold and calculating, becoming too theoretical does not make for a youth work practice that enables warm and respectful relationships with young people to be built up.

So, we have to maintain a balance between this, and the risk of not trying to understand these gut feelings at all. To write a book about youth work that hopefully explains things, means trying to understand them in the first place. A parent will find it difficult to teach a child how to read unless they can read themselves, and a teacher will find it difficult to teach a child how to add up numbers unless they understand how to do it. Similarly, I cannot explain why some things in youth work seem to work better than others without trying to understand them myself. To explain your gut feelings, hunches and intuitions to others means having to understand where they come from in the first place.

Exactly the same argument applies to learning. If we have any interest at all in being better, more effective youth workers we need to be able to read, talk and think about what we do. If we do this we can benefit from others' experiences, clarify our experiences and improve and develop our practice.

Once again we do this all the time! We consider how things go in our work, we think of ways of improving them, and we talk and listen to other youth workers. All this is what academics mean when they talk about 'theory'. If we did not do this we would go on making the same mistakes again and again, we would always be restricted to the limitations of our own experiences, and we would not become better and more effective youth workers. In the case of the two young people getting edgy, we might try physical force to prevent things getting out of hand, or persuasion, or humour. If it works, it is informative to understand why it worked in that situation in order that we can use the same technique again to the same end. If intervention by force does not work we may have even better reasons for trying to understand why it didn't work – like a bloody nose! – in order to avoid things getting violent the next time.

Not to try to understand is to practise youth work by chance, to never know what is best to do and to always take the same shots in the dark. The result is an unprofessional, ineffective youth worker with no direction, no means of improving their practice, and probably a bloody

...we talk to other youth workers about our practice...

nose. The result is we have to walk a tightrope between the two extremes.

There is no set answer to where you might find your balance on this tightrope; how one youth worker balances will probably be different to another. Some youth workers lean towards the spontaneous, while others prefer the theoretical. In the end we have to find our own balance with our own combination of analysis and trial and error. We need both, since without either our abilities to perform are severely limited. To reject theory is to reject thinking; to reject hunches is to reject being human. We need to be humans that think. We have to make judgements, we have to follow hunches, but the more informed these judgements and the more understood the hunches, the better we are able to improve our practice.

Evaluation and reflection allows you to learn and develop your techniques through a never ending process of learning through your own experiences. Trying things out, evaluating their success and changing them as necessary, for example:

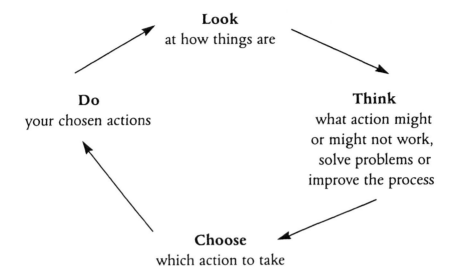

Look
at how things are

Do
your chosen actions

Think
what action might
or might not work,
solve problems or
improve the process

Choose
which action to take

In practice, sessions are likely to be planned beforehand but the youth worker will be ready to discard their plans if they seem inappropriate. They are rarely so sure of themselves that they will resist changing them as a result of changes in the circumstances or group.

They will always try to listen to feedback from the group and will rarely try and to themselves. If other people say they feel this or that way then it is important that this is treated with respect. If someone says that they feel patronised then they will try to accept that they do and adjust the way they work accordingly. They will try to listen carefully to what participants in the group say and feel so that they can get better at what they are doing.

They won't expect to get praised for their skill; after all, they want the group members to get on without them, so if group members say 'you were wonderful' or 'what would we have done without you?', then they might well feel that something is going wrong. They will also talk and explore their experiences with other youth workers, flick through the journals, and maybe even read the odd book if particular areas of their work need greater consideration.

So if the youth worker is going to achieve his or her objectives, exercise his or her power thoughtfully and carefully, and build up trust he or she will need to think about what he or she is doing and how effective it is. He or she will need to evaluate!

One more thing that youth workers will need to be aware of, and evaluate, is the context in which they are working.

6 The Context of Your Project

Youth work is not carried out in isolation. It takes place in a context. One perspective on the context – a wide one – is that youth work operates in a society divided along lines of class, race, gender, disability and sexuality. Youth workers need to recognise that they, and the young people they work for, live in a society such as this and so must ensure that their work does not support and attempts to challenge it.

Whatever we feel about this there is little we can do to change it in the short term, but we do have some control over the context and circumstances of the youth project itself.

In youth work that tries to make this context appropriate to the work the youth worker will be asking him- or herself questions about the whole atmosphere of the project he or she works in. Does it complement the process youth workers are trying to implement with young people? Are decisions taken openly and are young people's comments and contributions valued? Are there contradictions between the way the project is run and the way that the processes of group work, dialogue building and skill development operate? And as a result, are the wrong expectations created? Are young people in general encouraged to participate, discuss, and be active? This may mean at any time changes in the way the project is administered, changes in the way budgets are allocated, and changes in the way staff are appointed to complement rather than contradict the work.

Youth workers will be aware that resources may need adapting, such as typewriters that anyone can use, user-friendly telephone number lists, labels on stationery cabinets, clearly laid out information on how to book a minibus, how to hire camping equipment, and who to see about what. Consideration will have to be given to child care arrangements and access for those with disabilities.

On a more detailed level, youth workers will consider how the rooms are laid out, whether the chairs are in circles or lines, where the youth workers sit in relation to all the young people, and the best time of the day for groups to meet. The order of activities will need some thought so that young people are in a reflective mood at the right time and in an energetic mood at others. Activities will be planned on the basis of the opportunities for dialogue, group development and the exercising of skills, and not on convenience or the youth worker's particular hobbies.

Youth workers' particular hobbies

In addition to this, the youth worker will have to ensure that the managers understand what they are trying to do and the sort of support they will need. They will also need to consider how to develop their skills and abilities through training or mutual support groups.

When reading all this about power, trust, evaluation and contexts, it becomes clear what a delicate and skilful task effective youth work is, and it can be seen that it is something of an art form, something that cannot be acquired or developed overnight, something that has to be practised, and something that can never be perfected. However, this is not a reason to be put off. On the whole, people enjoy exercising skills, being in a group and taking part in dialogue, but the more skilful the worker, the better the results will be.

This is not easily achievable, but as the proverb says, 'aims are like stars, we never reach them but they guide us'. This book takes a similar approach in that we can see what we are aiming for but we also know from our experience how different the reality can be. In most youth projects the practice of youth work is less than ideal. The youth worker is harassed and ageing fast. He or she has a management committee that wants miracles performed, few resources and little professional support. More time is spent raising money, repairing damage, sorting out disagreements and sweeping up than actually doing youth work. The ideals that were developed on a youth and community course some years in the past seem a distant vision which it would be hard to remember if it wasn't for the occasional conference or training day which brings back the taste of inspiration. The day-to-day contact with young people is okay, but always overshadowed by the other pressures. When groups and activities go well that feeling of hope returns but when they go badly it once again seems a million miles away. There is always that feeling that things would be fine if only we could just... The youth worker knows that young people benefit from the project, but finds it hard to explain this to others and sometimes even to him- or herself.

This feeling will have resonance with many youth workers and this book may seem idealistic when viewed in these terms. However, we don't think that the sort of groups you are working with and the contexts you are working in are going to be that straightforward, and in reality the suggestions in this book are likely to be used in bits and pieces, as and when the circumstances allow. What is important is that whatever the circumstances, objectives such as those outlined in this book are not ignored or forgotten. All of us work in circumstances that are hardly conducive to perfect youth work, but what we do achieve – the skills, values, understandings and beliefs, and confidence that young people do develop – are largely the result of the work we do manage to squeeze in between the chaos, crisis and paperwork.

The rest of this book is about putting this into practice. We look first at how the context of the youth work needs considering; then we look at the way a youth worker might work in practice; and then we consider how he or she is going to evaluate his or her work. Following on from this we look at the development of skills, taking each of the twelve core skills in turn and considering how youth workers might try to develop them in practice. We then look at dialogue and consider a number of different ways of building dialogue around a number of different topics. Lastly, we look at groups and the sort of issues that youth workers may need to deal with from time to time, and how these might be tackled.

There are three important things that need to be said about all this. The first is that these are not comprehensive, definitive lists of exercises and activities. There are many good books around looking at different aspects of youth work practice, and we are not intending to replicate them. We hope they will give you ideas and indicate the variety of ways you can deal with any area of youth work.

The second is that some exercises, methods, and approaches only work for some people. You need to find methods that you feel comfortable with, that suit your circumstances, and we do not want to suggest in the pages that follow that these are necessarily them. We do hope that some might suit you and that there will be enough ideas to trigger off more for your own personal repertoire.

The third is that the areas we cover are neither exclusive nor separate. They are the areas that we thought most useful but the possibilities are infinite, and you will find some more useful than others. In much the same vein the different areas often merge and overlap, and once again you should use them in the way that suits you and your circumstances.

Given these three provisos, we hope the book will be useful to you. Above all it is the little things that count – the combination of five minutes' dialogue, a few skills exercised and a good group activity that builds into transformative work. Out of little acorns...

Part Two

Putting it into Practice

7 Being the Youth Worker

GETTING THE CONTEXT RIGHT

The context that youth workers are operating in has a powerful influence on the sort of work they are able to do. The circumstances of each project are unique but there are two things that might be worth considering.

The first is whether the project or centre takes on the same objectives as you do in your youth work. Does the project itself welcome and encourage dialogue? Does it allow for and value young people exercising the core skills? Does it allow youth workers to work with groups? And does it offer the resources necessary for all this?

This is of importance for two reasons; one is that if it does not do these things then opportunities are being lost; the other is that if young people are used to one thing – to having activities organised for them, to having decisions being made for them, of not being included in dialogue – then they will find it harder to deal with things when they are asked to organise their own activities, make their own decisions and enter into dialogue. It is also important because youth work is difficult to do in isolation. We all need shoulders to cry on and hands to help us, and if our colleagues or our management do not share our approaches to youth work and value our practice we find ourselves struggling against the circumstances rather than working towards our objectives.

The second thing that might be worth thinking about is whether it allows you to do these things. Are the right sort of rooms available? Does the programme allow for such work? Does everyone have access to the building? Do those who need it have child care support? And do you have the resources you need to carry out your work effectively?

Both these things matter, but it is possible to meet groups at other venues, to take them where there are less distractions or to find support elsewhere. You have to find the best context for your work, but it does matter and it needs some consideration.

ROLE AND STYLE

What we are looking for is a youth worker with a particular role and style. Examples include:

- **The authoritarian youth worker,** who makes decisions and announces them, or presents decisions and sells them to the group, or presents decisions and invites questions or clarification.

- **The consultative youth worker,** who presents tentative decisions subject to change, or presents a situation, invites input and then makes a decision, or asks for a decision to be made but holds a veto over the outcome.

- **The enabling youth worker,** who defines limits, shares information and calls for a decision, or calls for the setting of limits, and initiates an exploration and decision making process.

It should be clear that the latter example, the enabler, is closer to the role that youth workers might be trying to work towards if they want to develop skills and build dialogue. The process of being an enabling youth worker might develop something like this:

1. A group is unhappy with something.

2. The youth worker stimulates them to think about what it is that is making them unhappy.

3. The group becomes aware of what it is that is making them unhappy but doesn't know what to do about it.

4. The youth worker helps them to think about what changes could be made that might help.

5. The group realises what changes could be made but doesn't know how to bring them about.

6. The youth worker helps the group to talk about how changes can be implemented.

7. The group decides how to implement these changes.

8. The youth worker supports the group in the implementation of changes.

9. The group is happy.

This process can be used over and over again if you keep in mind that unhappiness can mean not knowing, for example, how to make a decision, where to find something out, or how to negotiate. Thus the youth worker allows the group to exercise its skills for itself, make its decisions, take responsibility for them, use its skills and talents, generate its own energy and momentum, and take on its own personality and build dialogue.

Generally, then, there are a number of things that might be worth keeping in mind.

A youth worker should try to:

- observe what goes on in a group
- identify clearly the needs of that group
- learn ways of dealing with those needs
- practise those ways in different situations
- take people's feelings seriously
- listen to what people say
- listen between the lines
- listen to feedback
- create positive responses
- enable the group to function at its best
- set up safety nets to prevent a big fall.

A youth worker should try not to be:

- the hub of the wheel
- the head of the table
- the centre of attention
- the leader.

...take people's feelings seriously...

A youth worker is someone who tries to:
- be open to criticism
- give and take
- provide and share information
- observe
- evaluate
- encourage
- be supportive
- be unthreatening
- be respectful
- understand
- be patient
- give guidance
- be flexible
- be adaptive
- listen

- respond
- offer questions not answers
- concentrate on the process not the product
- offer options.

It is easiest to work with groups when:

- the group has ownership
- the group is motivated
- good relationships are established
- the circumstances are conducive to dialogue and skill development
- colleagues and management committees are supportive.

EVALUATING YOUR WORK

Evaluation is all about learning from your mistakes, appreciating your successes and developing your skills at youth work. To evaluate how things are going during a session:

- Ask and talk to people about it.
- Leave the group to sort out a problem on their own (think of an excuse to leave the room); do this every now and again and see how much better (or worse!) they are getting at organising themselves.
- Check that people are not staring out of windows.
- See if the members of the group are getting more confident.
- Check if any of the skills are being exercised.
- Check that there are opportunities for dialogue.

To evaluate how things are going outside a session:

- Write out a plan beforehand then write out what really happened and compare the two.
- Write out your vision for a group when you start working with them and after a few months reread it and think why it has or hasn't gone as you had hoped.
- Ask yourself and others:
  - Was enough time spent on…?
  - Was everyone able to take part?

...*are people staring out of windows?*

...*did you find what you expected?*

- What would be better next time?
- What was the best and worst thing about the session?
- Are people looking forward to the next session?
- Are the aims and objectives being achieved?
- Was the pace too fast or too slow?
- Did you find what you expected?
- Do members feel a part of the group?

8 Developing Skills

In the first part of this book we looked at the development of skills and we identified twelve that we suggested allowed the worker to be more specific and more aware of what he or she were trying to do. We emphasised that these skills are not prescriptive but skills that, at most, might form the core of your skill development work. They were:

1. the ability to assess your strengths and weaknesses
2. the ability to seek information and advice
3. the ability to make decisions
4. the ability to plan time and energy
5. the ability to carry through agreed responsibilities
6. the ability to negotiate
7. the ability to deal with people in power and authority
8. the ability to solve problems
9. the ability to resolve conflicts
10. the ability to cope with stress and tension
11. the ability to evaluate your own performance
12. the ability to communicate.

We explored how youth workers could develop these skills in their work and concluded that we would see:

- *young people* being in a position where they have to exercise the core skills for themselves
- *youth workers* planning programmes and activities where young people can exercise core skills.

- *young people* doing things for themselves
- *youth workers* explaining so young people understand how they can do things for themselves.

- *young people* being allowed to make mistakes
- *youth workers* ensuring that mistakes are not harmful.

- *young people* considering how effective their actions were
- *youth workers* encouraging this reflection.

- *young people* being able to use the skills in other circumstances
- *youth workers* helping young people see that the skills are valuable and transferable.

- *young people* recognising that they already have many of these skills to some degree or another
- *youth workers* valuing and crediting existing skills.

- *young people* exercising skills to a degree that they would not have done otherwise
- *youth workers* ensuring that young people are not frightened off by being asked to do too much.

This description is the background of this section on how to put this into practice. We look at the recognition and transference of skills and the twelve core skills themselves. Each section looks at particular sorts of tools that you might find useful, either to use as they are or to develop your own techniques. They are considered under 'Things to do and talk about'. This relates to the discussion in an earlier chapter where we argued that exercising a skill is only half of the process; reflecting upon and talking about how to do it and how it went is the other half.

It is left to you to decide which tools or exercises are going to suit you and the group you are working with, and when they might be used to greatest advantage. Above all you should view them as initial suggestions from which you can develop your own particular tools that best suit your circumstances.

RECOGNITION AND TRANSFERENCE OF SKILLS

(knowing what you have learnt and how to use it)

Introduction

There is little point in letting someone exercise their skills if they don't recognise:

- what skills they already possess
- what skills they are learning
- how they can use them in other circumstances.

This is a crucial part of developing these skills and you need to make the group aware that it is exercising and developing skills over and over again. Most people will regularly use most of the core skills but will not always recognise them as being valuable.

Things to Do and Talk About

- Use the group's own vocabulary when talking about skills.
- Always try to relate discussions to real life.
- Use the accessible definitions of the skills, such as those which are alongside the headings on each of the sections on the core skills.
- Use the examples in each section on the core skills to explain what the skill is.
- Mention that 'This is a skill that I use all the time in my work, and so and so uses it in his or her work'.
- Talk about any of the skills as often as you possibly can.
- At the start of a session talk about what they have, for example, negotiated for, made decisions about, or evaluated, etc., in the past.
- At the end of the session talk about when they are doing something like this again and how they might do it differently.

ASSESSING YOUR STRENGTHS AND WEAKNESSES

(knowing what you are good at, knowing what you are not good at, tasks are going to be easy, which ones are going to be hard)

Introduction

People need to have a realistic idea of what they are and are not good at. This can be difficult, particularly admitting that you might not be good at something, but equally many people's skills are unrecognised or unvalued, and consequently admitting that you are good at something can be as important.

It is not possible to get each member to appreciate and understand their strengths and weaknesses in one session; skills like this need to be developed over the whole project. It is possible to get them to experience the process of thinking about them and to recognise that one of the advantages of groups is that they have a wide range of strengths between the members.

Things to Do and Talk About

- Go through the possible tasks involved in the project; try to relate them to other tasks that individuals already do.
- Talk about those which they can do easily.
- Plan a session on each of the tasks that they feel they can't do.
- Encourage individual members to pass on their skills to the others.
- Try to relate the tasks that need doing for any given project to the twelve core skills.
- Make a general list of five things each individual thinks they are good and bad at.
- Make sure there is plenty of credit for skills already possessed.
- Avoid people saying they can do everything, or that they can do nothing.
- Talk about who can help them with the things they can't do.
- Talk about when they have said they can do something which they couldn't.
- Talk about when they said they couldn't and could.

- Talk about what things they have done well in the past and what things they have done badly.
- Talk about whether people are born with skills or acquire them.

...tasks you can do 'no sweat'...

Examples to Use

- Knowing whether you can do a job you want to apply for.
- Knowing what you might have to learn in order to apply for a job you want.
- Knowing what would be really useful to learn.
- Other people knowing that if you say you can do something, you can.
- Knowing when not to start something because you cannot finish it.

- Bettering yourself.
- Having a good feeling about yourself.
- Self-respect.
- Being able to be well prepared for anything you do.
- Being able to say you are good at something and not being big-headed.
- Having the confidence to say you are not good at something.
- Recognising and valuing the skills you have.

...knowing what would be really useful to learn...

SEEKING INFORMATION AND ADVICE

(knowing what to ask, knowing who to ask, working things out, checking things out, getting the facts, not being afraid to ask)

Introduction

This is a skill that can be built into almost every stage of a project. Some people see the seeking of information and advice as a failing, so make sure that it is seen as a valuable skill. Above all, people need to feel confident to be able to seek information and advice, and that means being well prepared as to what they want to find out and not worrying that they might feel stupid if they get something wrong.

Things to Do and Talk About

- Talk about who can manage without information and advice – no one knows everything!
- Where have they been before to get information and advice?
- What was it like?
- Who do they know already who would give them the information and advice?
- Use every opportunity to get individuals to seek information and advice.
- Try to get the group to visit the main sources during a project, i.e. library, advice centre.
- Start by seeking information and advice from places they know.
- Keep a list of contacts made during a project.
- Seek information from other people who have run similar projects.
- Link work into a list drawn up of strengths and weaknesses of things they need to know.

Finding out if you can get a loan from a bank...

Examples to Use

- Visiting a business advisory service.
- Going to an advice centre to sort out dole or housing problems.
- Going to a family planning unit about a pregnancy.
- Reading a car repair manual to fix a car.
- Going to a college to find out what courses you could do.
- Finding out if you can get a loan from a bank.
- Asking about rights on ET or YTS.

MAKING DECISIONS

(making up your mind, getting a real agreement, and sticking to it)

Introduction

Decisions and how they are taken are at the core of good group work practice. People need to feel that they have had a say in a decision – if they feel they were part of that decision then they will probably give more commitment and energy. It is often worth trying to use the same method of making decisions all the way through the project.

There are different ways that decisions can be taken in a group, for example:

- **The non-decision.** Here the group makes a decision by not making a decision. 'Not to decide is to decide'. Someone makes a suggestion, but it drops like a stone and no one pays any attention to it at all. If the person who made the suggestion really felt enthusiastic about it, the fact that it was totally ignored could make that person withdraw or resist later suggestions. They will certainly feel undervalued and they might have very good reasons for making that suggestion that no one else has thought of. It may well be that this is the result of social divisions such as gender or race.

- **The one-person decision.** This is quickly made, but later when the decider depends on free or voluntary support from others to implement it, he or she may find him- or herself carrying it out alone. This might be the facilitator making this decision.

- **The unquestioned decision.** One person makes a suggestion. Another says 'What a great idea', and without further discussion the matter is decided. These decisions are more frequent than one thinks, and often pass unnoticed at the time, but the resentment comes to the surface later.

- **The clique.** This decision is made by a small group who plan beforehand to get their way. Because they are better organised than those who disagree, they are often successful on the immediate issue, but they bring a spirit of rivalry rather than cooperation into the group.

- **The minority decision.** These decisions are not as consciously organised as those of the clique, but a few powerful personalities dominate the group. Often this is unconsciously done, and then later they wonder why others are apathetic.

- **The majority vote.** In big groups this is often the most effective way to make a decision. However, one may lose the interest or the loyalty of the minority who voted against a decision, especially if they feel their point of view was not heard or they felt very strongly about the issue.

- **The silent consensus.** Some groups aim at unanimous decisions. These are good, if genuine, but they can rarely be achieved on important issues. Unanimous agreement is sometimes assumed when some members have not felt free to disagree and have kept silent.

- **The consensus.** This is an agreement, often involving compromise or the combination of various possibilities, after all opinions have been heard. Disagreements and minority viewpoints are fully discussed. It takes care and time to build a climate in which all feel free to express themselves, but this method does build unity, cooperation and commitment. It does not mean listening to people and then doing what we were going to do in the first place. It means adapting to accommodate the concerns of all. It may take longer to make a decision this way, but it will often be carried out more quickly and wholeheartedly.

Things to Do and Talk About

- Hold a secret ballot to sound out opinion; it creates interest but should be done after discussion, and should not be final. It can be useful to initiate a discussion on whether a consensus or majority decision should be used. Score preferences especially on multiple option decisions, i.e. each scores out of ten how much they favour each option. Add up the totals and discuss the results. This can allow people a degree of anonymity, and can be done before and after discussion, and the results compared. Ask what would be needed to raise one score or lower another.

- Try the 'NASA Exercise', where members are told that they are part of the crew of a space ship travelling across the surface of the moon. The ship crashes 200 miles from the base. The following items have survived from the crash and the members need to rank them in order of importance to help them survive the trip back to base:

  1. box of matches
  2. food concentrate
  3. 50 feet of nylon rope
  4. parachute silk
  5. portable heating unit
  6. two .45 pistols
  7. case of dehydrated milk
  8. two 100-pound tanks of oxygen
  9. stellar map

10. life raft

11. magnetic compass

12. five gallons of water

13. light flares

14. first aid kit

15. solar FM radio.

NASA's answer is: oxygen, water, map, food, radio, rope, first aid kit, parachute silk, life raft, light flares, pistols, milk, heating unit, compass, and matches. Most of the rankings are fairly self-explanatory, but out of interest, the parachute silk is selected to protect survivors from the sun's rays; the life raft is selected because the carbon dioxide bottles might be useful for propulsion and the same reason is given for the .45 pistols; and the radio is given a low priority because FM only has a short range.

Ask the group to list their priorities individually and then get them to draw up one list collectively. Does the more dominating member's list tally with the group list? Is the quietest one's list completely different from the group one? How was the group list drawn up? Did everyone have a say? Did someone take the role of chairperson? Did someone take on the role of secretary?

Remember the reason for doing this exercise is not to get the NASA answer, although the participants are likely to be interested in this, but to use the answers that are arrived at individually and collectively to discuss how the group made collective decisions and to discuss this.

- Talk about a decision that has already been made and how it was taken, e.g. how long the meeting should be, which night to meet.
- Ask about better and worse ways that could have been used.
- Ask about information needed to make this decision.
- Use the 'But why' method of questioning a decision.

    Q. How often should we meet?

    A. Monthly.

    Q. But why?

    A. Because we don't want to meet weekly.

Q. But why?

A. Because we think meetings are boring.

Q. But why?

A. Because we just get talked at.

Q. But why?

Is the quietest one's list completely different from the group one?

- Ask how we should make decisions.
- Ask how you would make decisions about, where to go in the evening, who's turn it is to buy the drinks, or who to vote for at an election.

Examples to Use

- Deciding whether to go on the Enterprise Allowance or not.
- Deciding which project to do.
- Deciding whether to apply for a job or not.
- Choosing where to go for your holidays.

- Deciding where to go for a trip.
- Deciding where to go for an evening out.
- Deciding what activities a girls' group is going to do.

PLANNING TIME AND ENERGY

(what comes first, what is the most important thing to do, what can be left until last)

Introduction

Planning time and energy is another skill that will crop up throughout the project. People need to understand that there are many small components to a project and each one has to be dealt with; they need to be able to plan without over-committing themselves and to work to a deadline.

Try to ensure that the horrible jobs don't get left to the last minute and that difficult or easy and boring or interesting tasks get shared out fairly. Having a well thought out plan helps to concentrate the group's energy in one direction.

Things to Do and Talk About

- Draw up a plan for the whole project.
- Divide it into weeks and tie it in with the skills that were discussed under 'Strengths and Weaknesses'.
- Look at the plan for each week and begin to allocate tasks.
- Get everyone to score out of ten what is the most important thing to do.
- Add up the totals and discuss the results.
- Draw up an individual's private timetable as it is at present, and see where he or she will fit in work on the project.
- Draw up a chart with columns headed 'now', 'soon' and 'later'; allocate tasks to columns.
- Update this chart each week.
- Ask about the fastest possible way to complete the work properly.

- How do members plan their time and energy now?
- Talk about the allocation of tasks in relation to the discussion held under 'Strengths and Weaknesses'.

Examples to Use

- Being efficient at work.
- Making the best use of your time.
- Getting things done to a deadline.
- Organising yourself to carry out any group of tasks, e.g. shopping, phone calls, visits, meals, all in a set amount of time.
- Organising your own activities.
- Planning a meeting.

CARRYING THROUGH AGREED RESPONSIBILITIES

(doing what you said you would do, getting on with things, being dependable)

Introduction

Groups depend on their individual members carrying out their agreed tasks. The key objective in such a session is that the individual members of the group understand clearly which tasks they have agreed to do and that the group depends on them to do them. Failure by one member to carry through an agreed task could result in the whole project being held up, and for this reason it is important to be aware that if the project is going well failure might result in considerable resentment and frustration from the rest of the group.

Consequently, you need to be careful that individuals take on tasks that they are capable of, and that those who might be more sensitive to resentment from the rest of the group succeed in their tasks, even if you have to help them. You need to be sensitive to whether criticism from the other group members would help or not.

Carrying out tasks is a good test of commitment and, over a period of time, is a good indication of how confidence is growing.

Things to Do and Talk About

- Try to let people choose their own tasks.
- Try to relate the tasks to the core skills.
- Keep a list of allocated tasks to refer back to at the next meeting.
- Check through it each week.
- Work in pairs or small groups so that people have support and encouragement from their partner or group.
- Talk about how the group will feel if someone lets them down.
- Talk about who did and who did not carry out their agreed task.
- Talk about how can we ensure tasks are done.
- Ask if we need to get help.
- Ask 'When have you agreed to do something for someone and let them down?'
- Ask 'When have you agreed to do something for someone and they have been able to depend on you?'
- Ask 'When has someone else agreed to do a task and let you down?'
- Ask 'When has someone else agreed to do a task and not let you down?'
- Talk about what might be good reasons for not doing something.
- Talk about how we can make constructive criticisms that do not offend but help.
- Talk about how we can take constructive criticisms without feeling hurt or put down.

Examples to Use

- Your ability to carry out a job given to you by your employer.
- Friends can depend on you.
- Turning up when you said you would.
- Finding out something you said you would find out.

NEGOTIATING

(wheeling and dealing, striking a bargain, getting the best possible deal)

Introduction

The essence of successful negotiating is the ability to understand the other party's viewpoint; without this understanding you are just taking pot shots in the dark. This makes this a good session for talking about what other people feel and want. Try to get participants to put themselves in other people's shoes and recognise that other people may have different values, beliefs, understandings, needs and wants.

The essence of successful negotiating is the ability to understand the other party's viewpoint...

Things to Do and Talk About

- Ask 'What does the group ideally want out of this negotiation?'
- Ask 'What does the other party ideally want out of this negotiation?'

- Ask 'Where should the group start bargaining from?'
- Ask 'What are we prepared to give to satisfy the other party's requirements?'
- Talk about things that they have recently negotiated for.
- Talk about how they might have done it better.
- Talk about the difference between bludgeoning or threatening someone into submission, and negotiating.
- Talk about whether the group can risk refusal.
- Talk about what restrictions are on the other party.
- Talk about how power might affect negotiation.
- Talk about how important it is to listen to what people are really saying.
- Offer to make the coffee in return for something else, then talk about what would happen if they refused to keep their side of the agreement.
- Use this session to draw up a contract.
- A good subject to do a role play on is to act out the parts of boss and employer negotiating wages or something similar.
- Write out six of the animals from the awkward members section and talk about how the group would negotiate with each type
- Get the group to get letters of support from the community to be submitted with applications for funding. It may be possible to persuade potential funders to sit down and negotiate the funding with the group. It is a very effective way of bringing in negotiation.

Examples to Use
- Negotiating to buy a motorcycle.
- Getting a landlord to carry out improvements.
- Borrowing something from a friend.
- Deciding where to go on an evening.
- Persuading someone to babysit.
- Persuading staff to keep the youth club open an extra hour.

DEALING WITH PEOPLE IN POWER AND AUTHORITY

(them and us, people in charge, sorting out the big cheese)

Introduction

Dealing with people in power and authority is one of the most useful skills for many young people to learn. Try to get the participants to recognise power for what it is, i.e. what is the root of someone's power and why do they have it? It is important that people recognise that power is not an exclusive property. For example, a councillor may have power over a youth project but the local young people have some power over him or her because he or she is dependant on them and their peers and families for votes. So power can operate both ways.

Many participants see this as the most useful skill they acquire in their particular projects.

Things to Do and Talk About

- Think of those in power in their underwear.
- Try to match whoever they are dealing with with one of the animals from the awkward members section. Talk about how the group would deal with them.
- Another good subject to do a role play on is, for example, arguing with a traffic warden, policeman or policewoman.
- Ask group members if getting angry would help.
- Talk about how they might deal with potential funders.
- Talk about why they might support the application.
- Talk about why they might reject the application.
- Talk about how they are going to persuade people to write letters of support.
- Talk about whether people should accept authority.
- Talk about what 'lobbying' is.
- Talk about forms of power (see Chapter 4).

Examples to Use

- Dealing with a counter clerk.
- Trade unionists negotiating a pay rise.

- Coping with hassle from parents.
- Coping with hassle from the police.
- Having authority over people at work.
- Having power over younger brothers and sisters
- Arguing with a social worker.
- Coping with youth and community workers.
- Dealing with a careers or housing officer.

PROBLEM SOLVING

(sorting things out, overcoming obstacles, finding a solution)

Introduction

The main objective in this session is to create some sort of understanding as to how people sort out problems. It is also worth discussing
how some problems are within your control and some are not. Remember that *they* need to solve the problem, not you.

Things to Do and Talk About

- Analyse a problem through the 'But why?' method on page 80–81.
- Break the problem down into its component parts.
- List possible solutions to each part.
- List the good and bad points of each possible solution.
- Brainstorm as under the section on ideas.
- Ask what the core of the problem is.
- Ask what someone they all know who deals with problems would do.
- Talk about problems they have had in the past.
- How did they solve them?
- Was it effective?

Examples to Use

- Changing modules on YTS.
- Coping when you don't get your Giro.
- Paying off debts.
- Getting repairs done to your flat or house.
- Sorting out problems with family and friends.
- Working out how to repair a pool table.
- Sorting out childcare regulations.

RESOLVING CONFLICTS

(not fighting things out, getting over disputes)

Introduction

The main objectives of this session are first, to get some recognition that it is worthwhile for the group to resolve conflicts and not let them split the group or fester, and second, to develop some understanding of how conflicts arise and are solved. These require a recognition that conflicts are inevitable but unresolved conflicts may not be.

Resolving conflicts makes for an easier, more comfortable life and group. Sometimes conflicts are such that a group reaches a point of no return and does split up. This may not be such a bad thing and you and the group need to learn from this experience.

Things to Do and Talk About

- Start by looking at both sides of the dispute and discussing the limits on which people might be prepared to accept compromise.
- Ask 'Does this mean the end of the project?'
- Talk about the aim again to confirm reasons for resolving the conflict.
- Talk about all the work that has been done up to now.
- Talk about whether the conflict needs to be resolved.

...sorting out arguments over youth club activities...

- Talk about what will happen if resentment builds up.
- Talk about how important it is that we listen carefully to what people are saying and don't jump to conclusions.
- Get group members in pairs and get each to put one hand on a pen and jointly draw a picture of a house. Talk about how they decided where to draw the lines.

- Get each side of the conflict to select fi   ai favour of their point of view.
- Get the two sides of the conflict to argue the other's point of view.
- If a discussion is getting fraught . . . get everyone to sum up what the previous speaker said before they say what they want to say.

Examples to Use

- Smoking or not smoking in meetings.
- Resolving a row between friends.
- Resolving a row in the family.
- Resolving a row over a pool table.
- Sorting out arguments over youth club activities.

COPING WITH STRESS AND TENSION

(not getting really pissed off, being got at, not panicking)

Introduction

Everyone suffers from some stress and tension at times, and the important thing in this session is to get individuals to appreciate that stress and tension happen, that they are uncomfortable feelings, but that they can be dealt with. It is important that you are sensitive to stress and tension and that you help people cope with them rather that let them go under.

Usually stress and tension are the result of some problem(s), so solving these will alleviate the stress and tension. They are also a confirmation that the individuals are committed and enthusiastic, so don't see it as all bad.

Psychological studies have shown that the simple perception of being in control is enough to alleviate stress, so emphasise the strengths and positive things that the group have done. Also, stress can be a good thing, as it gets the adrenalin going and makes the individual perform better.

Things to Do and Talk About

- Talk about what exactly it is that is causing the stress and tension.
- Talk about what the worst outcome would be.
- Talk about whether the issue is worth getting stressed about.
- Talk about how stress affects people, i.e. feeling sick, angry, frustrated, disappointed, worried.
- Talk about when they have felt that way before.
- Talk about what they did about it.
- Talk about how well that worked.
- Break the problem down into little bits.
- Make sure that everyone feels responsible for whatever it is that is causing the stress.
- Work in pairs to boost individual confidence.
- Use role play to act out dreaded situations before they occur.

Examples to Use

- Not worrying that your giro won't come and you can't pay off a debt.
- Not worrying that you might not get the job you've just been interviewed for.
- Not getting depressed.
- Not bottling things up.

EVALUATING YOUR PERFORMANCE

(knowing how well you did, what went wrong, learning from your mistakes)

Introduction

It is important in this session to develop some sort of understanding about why it is important to evaluate your progress. It is important to maintain a balance between the negative and the positive for each individual, and evaluation also provides the facilitator with excellent feedback on their facilitation. An evaluation session can help bring the project to a conclusion, rather than it just petering out, and a report back to the funders can also be useful. One of the best ways to learn is through your mistakes.

Things to Do and Talk About

- Write out a genuine 'to whom it may concern' reference for each participant at the end of the project.
- Go through the contract if you wrote one out.
- Go through the scrap book if you kept one.
- If the project was for someone else's benefit then get their opinions.
- Make a list of good and bad points about the project.
- Get everyone to say what they think the person sitting next to them thought about the project.
- Look back at the list drawn up in 'Strengths and Weaknesses' and see if anything has changed.
- Look at the core skills and get participants to gauge, on a scale of one to ten, how good they were at the beginning of the project and how good they are now at things like working in a group, or planning time and energy. It may be worthwhile to do this yourself in each case and compare results with them.
- Talk about what they would do differently if we did it again.
- Talk about what complaints or compliments people would like to make.
- Talk about what the best parts were.
- Talk about what the worst parts were.
- Talk about what the biggest problem was.
- Talk about what the hardest task was.
- Talk about how they were evaluated at school, work, or YTS.
- Talk about your performance as a facilitator.

EXAMPLES TO USE

- People who say they are good at things and aren't.
- Not applying for a job you cannot do.
- Not bragging.

- Not being over modest.
- Looking back at things realistically.
- Being receptive to criticism.
- Learning a trade.
- Bringing up kids.

COMMUNICATING

(talking to people, letting them know what you think, listening to what others think)

Introduction

Communication is an essential skill and of all the core skills is the one that groups will most readily recognise that they have and use.
Communication is most effective when:

- you are sure of what you say
- things are put in a logical order
- people are in the right frame of mind
- the subject is of interest
- the vocabulary is appropriate
- it is two-way.

This skill is exercised throughout the whole project and although there are some exercises below that you might want to try, your main concern should be that the group recognises that they are using this skill and that it is valuable.

Things to Do and Talk About

- Ask when they have been misunderstood.
- Ask what the result was.
- Talk about times when someone may have insulted someone else without meaning it.
- Talk about anything that affirms the value of communication.
- Talk about how advertisers communicate a message.
- Play Chinese Whispers. The facilitator whispers a message of about twenty words to the first member of the group, who

whispers it to the second member, who whispers it to the third, and so on, until it gets to the last member of the group who repeats the message out loud. This is likely to be very different from the original message and is useful for discussing how important communication is. The whisper can only be repeated once to each person.

- Get group members to repeat a point of view that someone has just expressed; how accurate were they? Were they listening?
- Discuss any misunderstandings that arise.
- Use words from race/gender/sexuality/disability/class stereotypes. Find out different definitions and meanings.
- Draw a pattern of six squares on a piece of paper; they can be at any angle but should be touching each other. Then get one of the members of the group to look at it and try to explain to the others how to draw it for themselves; without looking and with only verbal instructions. It is a surprisingly difficult thing to do and is a good illustration of communication skills.

Examples to Use

- Not saying the wrong thing at a job interview.
- Explaining your case at the housing office.
- Not getting in a temper because someone doesn't understand you.

9 Building Dialogue

Earlier in this book we looked at why building dialogue was important and what sort of situation we were looking for if we were to maximise the opportunities for this happening. The situation we described was where:

- *young people* are able to explore their values, beliefs and understandings
- *youth workers* create circumstances where this is valued and encouraged.

- *young people* look under the surface of their values, beliefs and understandings
- *youth workers* offer information, experiences and facilitation to enable this to happen.

- *young people* have the freedom to explore their values, beliefs and understandings in any direction
- *youth workers* are sensitive to the varying strands of thought that might emerge but may look for opportunities to guide the dialogue in a particular direction.

- *young people* do not feel they have to cling to their values, beliefs and understandings
- *youth workers* build up a maximum level of trust and respect to help young people to feel comfortable about taking risks.

- *young people's and youth workers'* values, beliefs and understandings are treated with respect but equally are open to question
- *young people and youth workers* contribute towards a shared exploration, an investigation, a 'community of enquiry'.

It may well be the case that these circumstances will come about on their own accord, but this is not likely and in most instances youth workers will be exercising their power to make it happen as often as possible. The rest of this section explores ways that this might be brought about, and looks at creating the right circumstances, building dialogue, and the tools for building dialogue.

CREATING THE RIGHT CIRCUMSTANCES

Creating the right circumstances involves a great number of considerations. If we set ourselves the task of creating circumstances where there is respect, where anything is open for discussion, where people are open minded and able to accept criticisms, and where young people feel free to express their opinions, then it is important to recognise that these

...creating the right circumstances...

conditions need to be created throughout the whole project and not just in an isolated session. For this reason it may be worth rereading the section of this book on getting the context right.

However, even when a project develops these themes through all its work, it is still worth giving some thought to the particular requirements of building dialogue. Circumstances in which dialogue building seems more successful include:

- **After participating in some physical activity** – for example, on the way back from a swimming trip, sitting round a camp fire after a day hillwalking, cleaning up after a disco, having a cup of tea after a tiring meeting planning a girls' day, late in the evenings.

- **As part of a practical activity** – for example, while hillwalking, while designing posters to advertise a girls' group, while mending the disco equipment, while playing pool, while doing arts and crafts.

- **Where there are no distractions** – for example, not next door to the disco, not in the same room as the pool table, not during an activity, not when the telephone is going to keep ringing, not when the lads are going to shout through the letterbox at the girls' group.

- **Where people feel at ease** – for example, in chairs that are not too uncomfortable but are not so comfortable that people fall asleep, somewhere that young people are used to, not somewhere where the formality is oppressive.

- **Where a high level of trust has been developed** – for example, after relationships and groups have had a chance to develop (see section on building trust).

Youth workers will rarely be able to create a set of ideal circumstances, as even the best of intentions are disrupted by all sorts of factors which cannot be anticipated, but progress down this road is possible if you try to plan for:

- the appropriate sorts of activities where dialogue can be included
- a timetable that minimises distractions and gives time for talking
- energetic activities with time set aside afterwards for talking
- a physical space that is conducive to dialogue

- increasing opportunities for dialogue as the group develops and trust grows.

BUILDING DIALOGUE

In the building of dialogue youth workers are trying to walk a tightrope. It involves getting the right balance between allowing young people to explore and discover things for themselves and providing the information and structure necessary for such an exploration to be informed and effective. In the real world of youth work any building of dialogue that does come about is going to be at a fairly informal, unstructured level. This does not negate the gains to be made through dialogue and it does not change the factors that youth workers should consider if they want to make it as effective as possible.

Over time the youth worker should be looking for opportunities and means to increase the opportunities for a group to:

...exercise intellectual facilities...

- **Talk** – encouraging the group to make its own decisions, telling them about dilemmas the project faces, asking questions.

- **Exercise intellectual faculties** – asking them about dilemmas, values, beliefs and understandings.

- **Adopt appropriate rules and procedures** – deciding where to hold sessions, when to end, and when and how people can interrupt; insisting on everyone having a say; and deciding what is on the agenda, and vocabulary appropriate to the group.

- **Develop their skills at group discussion** – asking people to give reasons for their statements, asking the group for its ideas for activities, asking the group about their views on the project.

- **Learn about other individuals in the group** – getting people to value the comments of others, asking individuals to explain their views, talking about issues such as race, gender, and politics, talking about why two views might be different, asking people to relate stories about their experiences.

- **Accept criticism** – questioning people's statements, getting people to see the value of criticism.

- **Explore things in some depth** – asking people for the reasons behind a statement, pointing out fallacies, feeding in appropriate information, encouraging the formation of more coherent values, beliefs and understandings, talking about how this change might affect them, discussing their character, the direction of their lives, other people around them, and society at large.

- **Listen to other group members** – reiterating a point someone made that was ignored the first time round, reinforcing a point made by someone else, asking individuals what they think of someone else's statement and asking for their reasons.

This requires the right sort of role for the youth worker, who needs to:

- Question the opinions and views of young people while at the same time treating them with respect.

- Try to make the dialogue enjoyable and interesting while at the same time tackling important issues.

- Offer enough information to inform the discussion but still allow young people to work things out for themselves.

- Allow enough freedom so that young people have some control over the direction, content and style of the dialogue but still

...explore things in some depth...

manage to build in issues and questions that he or she wants to see discussed.

• Contribute to but not dominate a discussion.

'...that is the essence of science: ask an impertinent question, and you are on the way to a pertinent answer.' (Bronowski 1973)

TOOLS FOR BUILDING DIALOGUE

Introduction

The list of possible issues about which dialogue can be built is, of course, endless. The best examples are often very localised and firmly rooted in the experiences of the young people you are working with. Dialogue is a process of education which increases the understanding of the individual but also improves the choices and life chances of others.

In order to begin to consider the issues affecting others we need to be aware of ourselves and how we organise ourselves and are organised by others. Before white young people can begin to understand racism, before people without physical or mental disability can begin to understand disability, and before young men can begin to understand young women, it is important that they recognise their own feelings, limitations, aspirations and fears. To this end it is important to consider building dialogue around self-understanding and acceptance as a basis for the understanding and acceptance of others. Two example methods might prove useful.

1. 'What makes me feel big and what makes me feel small.' This exercise works very well with young people and can be used successfully with adult groups, too. It enables an understanding of self-worth versus intimidation by illustrating how individuals feel in day-to-day situations.

    Two lists are made, one entitled 'What makes me feel big', the other 'What makes me feel small'. It is inevitable that with discussion each 'What makes me feel small' list will include name calling or personal criticism. In allowing recognition for how you feel yourself when called 'slag', 'spaka', or 'poofter', it is natural to move on to 'How do you think others feel when you call people names?'. This can then be developed to consider situations of racism, sexism, poverty, sexuality, and so on.

    For a lasting effect posters can be made of the combined lists. In effect they become the ground rules for how the group's members treat each other and increasingly there is an awareness that allowing and encouraging the positive actions in the 'What makes me feel big' list permits a greater freedom for all whilst increasing individual and collective self-worth and confidence.

2. Identify situations in which young people feel ill at ease, left out, or threatened by the actions or language of others. Encourage young people to identify when they feel comfortable and uncomfortable. How do they act or react? Where do they feel most and least comfortable? Who are they with in these situations? It will emerge that they feel least threatened and most confident when they are with their friends, on their own patch,

using their own language, and discussing things which are relevant to them.

They feel most threatened and least confident when alone, in unusual surroundings, using others' language, and in situations where they feel unfairly judged because they are young or because of their appearance. This can be highlighted by reminding young people of situations they have been in, e.g. calling at the civic centre for information, visiting another part of town or the country or the world, or being one young person amongst a lot of older people. Again it is vital that having recognised situations in which they feel insecure, they consider how others might feel in similar circumstances; a person without a disability who is on public transport, for example, or someone from another country who cannot understand English very well, or someone who speaks English with a different accent. What we are trying to do is to get young people to understand culture, the power of being in a dominant culture and the powerlessness of being in a minority culture.

'As a member of a dominant culture, or when working in your own culture, the normal illusion is that your reality is everybody's reality. You see your system as 'how things are', and expect everyone else to fit, since you 'know best'. When you are in somebody else's culture, things are different. You are the one who's out of sync. you may feel shy. wrong, guilty, stupid or ashamed, even though you are doing your best to understand.' (Simons 1989)

These examples for allowing young people the freedom to express themselves and therefore enter into a dialogue are basic and simple, and the examples which follow will be equally attainable. In order for workers to be able to respond to issues as they arise and to introduce issues they must look for tools which are around them and which young people have easy access to. Initially dialogue needs to be developed in a small or perhaps seemingly insignificant way, and built on slowly, bringing external stimuli and events when young people are practised at looking at their own experiences and actions.

Each of the areas we have identified to build dialogue around is extremely complex. A worker must be aware of their own value base and the extent of their own prejudices before tackling change in others. The worker must be willing to change their views, increase their knowledge and explore their own experience for dialogue around these issues to be productive.

Effective dialogue relies heavily on resourcefulness. Comments, ideas and feelings must be picked up and used to develop further comment, new ideas and an understanding of feelings. This resourcefulness is very individual but relies on the youth worker being able to collect and use the relevant tools. These will generate and stimulate new directions for the thoughts of participants and essentially encourage young people to question what they have, until now, believed to be true or normal. It is sometimes necessary to use specific methods to shift the direction or level of discussion to ensure that young people are challenging the thoughts and views of themselves and each other.

Using Resources

The following are examples of resources which have been used in the past and have been useful in creating dialogue. It is possible that they may be useful in specific circumstances in which you find yourself, although it is more likely that they will illustrate the wide range of resources which are usable and the myriad of issues which arise from the constructive use of tools which are readily available.

VIDEOS

These are usually expensive, too long and require an audience which is already motivated towards the topic. It is sometimes possible to play the video as background in the hope that someone will pick up on the issues it raises. When used casually and informally they can be an ideal tool for dialogue.

Disability – Changing Practice (Dant and Quinn 1990a) is a video which forms part of an Open University Course on disability. The video is divided into short usable sections. 'A Saturday Night Out' lasts for three and a quarter minutes and highlights the range of barriers which inhibit disabled people from enjoying themselves and organising their own lives.

The showing of this video might be followed up with questions such as:

- Where do you see people with disabilities?
- Where don't you see them?
- Why don't you see them?
- What stops people with disabilities going into pubs, theatres, cinemas, nightclubs, youth centres?
- Where do people you know with disabilities go?
- How do people react?
- Why don't we want disabled people to enjoy themselves?
- What should be done to make it possible for them to be able to act as they want?

It may also be followed up by looking at and talking about cartoons like the one by Sophie Grillet from *Disability – Changing Practice* by Tim Dant and Geraldine Quinn (1990a).

CURRENT AFFAIRS

These are easy to introduce and are usually things which it is possible to get opinions on. Initially it is best to use very localised current affairs, including any items of local news or events such as crime, fights, changing a pub name, closing a shop, or building a road. It is usually possible to get an account of what is happening and often a simplistic view of whether it is right or wrong, or whether someone agrees or disagrees. It is often more difficult to consider why something is happening or why someone holds the view they do. It is at this point that dialogue begins. Local events are often difficult to pursue if someone feels it is nothing to do with them or none of their business. You must be conscious that your desire to build dialogue may be interpreted as snooping or gathering information which is not yours to have.

Wider examples of current affairs can involve anything of national interest, such as the pit closures, the Royal family, or funding of political parties. Although the easiest way to generate a level of discussion, young people are often repeating what they have heard or read and this doesn't mean they are entering into a dialogue with you. It is thus often necessary to intervene with such direct questions as: 'Do you think that...?', 'What difference would it make if...?', 'Who told you that?', 'Did you read that somewhere?'.

Use photographs from papers, and quotes from 'famous' and/or local people.

POSTERS

These can be used continually and there are many which are produced specifically to make young people think as well as to pass on information or facts. For posters to be effective it is important to know why you are using them. Often they are used for decoration and never referred to. If the same posters are left up for too long they lose their impact. There are sets of posters which can be used together, and others which give the same message in different ways. They are usually relatively cheap and often free, especially ones which fall into the health promotion category which if used creatively can be ideal for initiating dialogue. Usually posters are not used but merely pinned up; they often lend themselves to witty additions being made by young people, and are occasionally used as a way to be anonymously racist, sexist or put across other oppressive views. This should be used as part of the exercise in dialogue building. Not *who* but *why* did someone write that? Is it funny? Who might not find it funny? Would you find it funny if you were black, or a woman?

These sorts of posters may lead to questions such as:

- What do you think of that poster?
- What is it telling us?
- Do you believe it?
- Why or why not?

GAMES

There are many games which are specifically designed for use with groups of young people. Some are designed for getting to know each other, and trust and confidence building; others for looking at specific issues and developing ideas and views. Confidence in introducing the game and encouragement to have a go usually results in young people not wanting to stop. Games are good ways of passing on factual information, generating discussion and having fun. It is possible for the continuation of the game to get in the way of dialogue, and sometimes so many issues are raised that it is not possible to develop them all. It is perhaps more realistic to use such games to highlight areas to return to at a later stage, and the first steps of dialogue will certainly be experienced.

For example, *Discoveries* is a board game produced by the YWCA of Great Britain to encourage young people to explore their values and beliefs.[1] The 'facilitator's checklist' says 'Participate but do not dominate, intervene as necessary, move the game on, support vulnerable players and get other players to support them, enable players to clarify what they are saying' – in other words, encourage dialogue.

The questions include a range of topics. Who should be responsible for looking after children?, How important is it to get along with people? What would you do if your partner hit you? Do you believe most religious people are hypocrites? Do you believe that morals and values in this country are bad and getting worse?

As a youth worker you must also be a player and it will often be necessary to pose questions, and to take an opposing viewpoint. For example, if everyone thinks religious people are hypocrites then it is necessary for you to explore why. Do they know any religious people? Are they hypocrites because they are religious? Why are religious people judged differently to other people? How do we expect religious people to behave? Do we excuse our lack of concern because of their behaviour? Each question begs many more and your judgement is your guide as to which to ask and expand on, and which to leave. You may want to use a game knowing it will bring up issues which need addressing. This can assist in moving an issue away from an individual to the relatively safe arena of a game. Young people can contribute more anonymously by answering questions asked of them by a game.

THE MEDIA

The media, TV and newspapers can be useful sources for dialogue on current affairs. But the TV is equally useful if used to discuss issues that arise from drama and soap operas. *Neighbours, EastEnders, Byker Grove, Casualty, The Bill* and many others offer opportunities to discuss many issues on young people's terms. It is certain that young people relate to these programmes and whilst they may not reflect their lives they do

---

1   Available from YWCA Headquarters, Clarendon House, 52 Cornmarket Street, Oxford OX1 3EJ.

tackle many of the issues facing young people including relationships, HIV/AIDS, pregnancy, divorce, unemployment, sexual abuse, sexual harassment, racism and so on. As well as discussing the events as they are happening, other issues should be raised.

The use of such material might result in asking such questions as:

- How are black people represented?
- How are young people portrayed?
- Are people with disabilities represented?
- How are heterosexual and homosexual characters portrayed?
- Why are condoms so rarely used on TV?
- What kind of picture is given of doctors, teachers, etc?
- Are the programmes realistic?
- What should be done to make them more or less realistic?

Advertisements are a further source of dialogue provided by the media. They are understandably blamed for much unrest in a materialistic society and it is important that young people are encouraged to question the messages they put across. Ask:

- How are women portrayed?
- What does the 'normal' home look like?
- How are black people and disabled people represented?
- How much money is spent on car adverts?
- How many cars are wrecked?
- Do adverts encourage you to want things?
- Are germs, dirt, smells and spots really so bad?
- Do chemicals, perfumes and potions really improve our lives?
- Did you know that tampons and sanitary towels can only be advertised after 9pm?
- Did you know that condoms cannot be advertised at all except as part of a health education message?

JOKES

Jokes are usually only useful to dialogue if you feel the time is right to discuss the 'humour' in racist, sexist or otherwise oppressive jokes. However, if you look and listen carefully there are jokes which can lead to dialogue. It is certainly possible to look at jokes in the light of why

...are germs really so bad?...

they are, or are not, funny. Again you are at risk of being unheard if you merely appear to lack a sense of humour.

Jokes might lead to you asking:

- Do you feel pressurised into laughing at jokes which you don't feel are funny?
- How often have you laughed because you know you are expected to?
- What reaction do you get if you say you don't think a joke is funny?
- What difference does it make to a joke to take out a racist reference and substitute it with 'a person'? For example, instead of 'There was an Irishman' simply say 'There was this person'.
- Can people with disabilities tell jokes about disability that people without disabilities cannot?
- Why is it attractive to us to laugh at other people?

- Are we simply attacking someone worse off than ourselves?
- Do jokes rely on understanding stereotypes?

There are many cartoons which are directed at young people; some are published as books of cartoons, while others are used as illustrations in magazines and journals. *You Worry Me Tracy, You Really Do!*, *He'd Be Quite Nice If*, and *Even My Gran* are by A. Martin (1987a, b, c) and are examples which young people, and especially young women, can relate to and can raise questions around relationships and how adults treat you. Following dialogue, many young people would be able to do their own cartoons.

...what reaction do you get if you don't think a joke is funny?

INTERESTING FACTS

These are clearly subjective, as what is interesting to me may be of no interest to you. However, such facts can often give a new insight into why we believe certain things to be true. Oppression and prejudice are based on fear and ignorance, and what is presented as fact is often simply an accepted 'truth' which has been repeated so many times that it is believed to be true. But it is not enough for us to simply question racist facts or sexist truisms; it is important to be able to produce new material which puts a different perspective on what is held to be true. A useful work might be *Black History for Beginners*, by Dennis and Willmarth (1984).

QUOTES

These are an interesting way to develop a dialogue starting from the point of 'What do you think this means?' For example, 'None of these people on the dole know what it's like to be in debt to half a million' (Jeffrey Archer), or 'We were told four years ago that 17 million people went to bed hungry every night. Well that was probably true – they were all on a diet' (Ronald Reagan).

Quotes can be used as sayings of the week, young people can contribute their own, posters can be made with photographs of young people and quotes underneath, calendars can be made for fundraising, and so on. Quotes can be from all sorts of people including pop stars, athletes, and politicians.

ACTIVITIES

Activities are important to the process of skill development and encourage young people to see the benefits of working as a group. They often offer opportunities to do new things and help young people see themselves in a new light. Activities are essentially only going to be a tool for dialogue if young people are encouraged to take responsibility for planning and organising and if they are given the opportunity to evaluate what happened and learn from their experience. A particularly useful resource for this is a book called *More than Activities* by Roger Greenaway (1990). It looks at planning, doing and evaluating activities with an emphasis on process.

QUIZZES

Quizzes are a fun way to pass on information and to assist young people in understanding their values and feelings and to form opinions. There are many ready made quizzes that appear in young people's magazines, often about relationships and how you would react in particular situations. *Young People Now* and *Youth Clubs* also often produce quizzes which are more issue-based. Alternatively, you can produce your own which can be more specific. It can be useful to use a quiz in conjunction with a series of posters which are being displayed; younger participants are especially motivated to discussion in this way. It is again essential to make sure that the questions lead to a dialogue. For example, the *New Internationalist* (November 1989) produced a questionnaire on heterosexuality called 'Do you Need Treatment?' which is extremely effective at encouraging acceptance of the existence of prejudice around homosexuality (*New Internationalist* 1989). It raises many important points about what is 'normal' and can of course be changed and adapted. Similar questions could be drawn up to look at racism and disability.

This particular quiz might lead to you to talking about:

- The part TV and newspapers have in determining what is considered 'normal'.
- Why homosexuality is seen as a threat.
- The difficulties for someone who is homosexual.
- Being frightened of things or people who are different.

EXPERIENCES

These should be the experiences of the young people which are often freely told when they involve bravado, amusing circumstances, danger or a challenge to authority. It is extremely skilful to be able to break into a round of stories, which get taller with each telling, with the aim of entering into a dialogue. It is also difficult not to get drawn into telling your own stories which, although they may be relevant and funny, will not necessarily lead to increased dialogue. It is however possible to use tools to encourage young people to talk about specific experiences which can lead to dialogue. There are many collections of young people's writing on subjects which are most relevant to young people's lives. These are a useful tool for dialogue if initially left for young people to read, borrow and discuss amongst themselves. The experience of reading them is the shared starting point for dialogue.

A collection such as *When People take the Mickey* (Rooney 1990), might lead to questions such as:

- Why do we make fun of others?
- How do we feel when it is done to us?
- When does teasing become bullying?
- Who has experience of being teased?
- Who has experience of being bullied?
- Who do you feel sorry for?
- What would you do if you saw someone being teased?
- If you are with a group who are bullying what do you do?
- Who is safest – the bullies or the bullied, and why?

- Do adults bully each other?

Another useful resource is the Livewire series of 'Books for Teenagers', published by The Women's Press.

All this illustrates the breadth of tools available for the youth worker and an indication of how he or she might use them. You will probably have your own stock of tools that you may use from time to time to initiate or build a dialogue. They can come in many forms and as with much else in youth work, you have to find ones that suit you and your style. On the whole, though, a good tool is one that:

- is interesting
- is enjoyable
- is stimulating
- is close to real life
- reveals questions as well as answers
- provides information.

These can be described as 'generative themes' or 'codes' in that they generate dialogue or they serve as codes through which we can decipher our world. Often a dialogue about any given topic will involve a process such as:

1. A description of what it is.

2. A discussion of it in a little more detail.

3. A discussion of how it relates to real life.

4. A discussion of how this relates to other things.

5. A discussion of what the root causes or explanations might be.

6. A discussion of what should be done about it.

What all these illustrate is the myriad of opportunities that youth workers may have to begin building dialogue, but also their need to be aware of their role in encouraging the delving under the surface without putting young people off by being too challenging, oppressive or dominating. Their role is clearly to help young people work these answers out for themselves.

What it also illustrates is that the discussion can go off at all sorts of tangents and it is partly up to the youth worker to decide, on the spot, which ones to take up and which ones to leave till later.

Topics and Resources

Introduction

Tools for dialogue, as we have seen, come in all shapes and sizes. What is important about these is that you use them to suit you and your circumstances. You know the young people you are working with, you know what might grab them, you know the way and the circumstances under which you work. So you have to choose the resources that are right for you. In the rest of this section we look at the resources we have come across that seem to work for certain topics.

We have seen that to build dialogue youth workers need an understanding of the subject under discussion, so youth workers need to be well informed about subjects that might interest young people. Below we look at resources that can be used for this and for generating dialogue with young people. Most of this section is divided up into subject areas but we start with a look at general resources.

GENERAL

Young People Now is published monthly by the National Youth Agency and is aimed at youth workers and young people. It carries a wide variety of articles including work being carried out, issue based information, recent news in the youth work world, and comment on government action and legislation which affect young people. It is both readable and attractive.

Youth Clubs is published monthly by Youth Clubs UK and the format is similar to *Young People Now*, although *Youth Clubs* is probably more attractive to young people. They have some good snippets of information and cover many of the issues as well.

Youth and Policy is a bimonthly journal published by a voluntary collective intended to share important theoretical developments with those working in the field. Some articles may be relevant, others may not. 'Working Space' offers the opportunity for workers to write their own thoughts, theories or analysis of their work. The more of us that contribute the more relevant it will become. Excellent reviews on books and resources. Read it! There is nothing better.

New Internationalist is a monthly magazine which has been published for years and looks at issues that the mass media and governments ought to be tackling. Issues relevant to youth work include education, housing, political activity, women, girls, children, racism, homosexuality, disability, poverty and many more, all from a global perspective. Lots of useful bits of information, quotes that are never heard or read in the news, and where possible a positive approach to educating people about vital issues. Excellent photographs, posters, diagrams, cartoons and other graphics. You really can't develop dialogue without it.

Oxfam Education provides a free catalogue, and if you live near one of their development education offices, visit them. Their material is cheap and very good and staff are sometimes employed to run sessions and courses. They have an almost endless supply of posters, leaflets, booklets and books on a whole range of relevant issues.

Newspapers are an endless source of material for dialogue. You need to be able to read one regularly which does not present an over-simplified, one-sided view of current affairs, because how can you explore under the surface if all you know is the superficial? However, this is only useful for building dialogue if you use it creatively. Less noteworthy papers can be useful when used as part of an overall discussion about what papers tell us or how they influence people, although it is impossible to justify having *The Sun* lying around because there are plenty of better resources which will be much more useful as a starting point. Some of the quality papers have education supplements which can often contain useful resources for building dialogue about all sorts of things.

Books – most of those listed in this book fall into three main categories: young people writing about their own experiences, training and workshop texts, and youth workers who have written either about their work or their shared good practice. So the majority are writing from experience and relating that experience for us to share, think about, discuss, agree with, disagree with or build upon. It is also important for youth workers to understand and acknowledge the theory that informs and underpins their work. Some of the texts mentioned do link the practice to theory but it is still important for youth workers to read more widely. The monthly journals already mentioned will provide some background but other reading should be an integral part of the youth worker's job.

THE COMMUNITY

Dialogue may include:

- What is a community?
- What purpose does a community serve?
- What role do children, young people, parents, family, and older people, play in a community?
- What affects the ability of a community to function positively? Housing? Crime? Employment? Transport? Schools?
- What do you need from your community?
- What do you put into your community?

Resources may include *Community Links Ideas Annual* by the Sheffield Women's Printing Co-op, (Community Links 1989, 1990, 1991), full of what other community groups have done in their communities, and lots of good ideas; also *The Charnwood Papers* by O'Hagan (1991), a series of papers on a variety of relevant topics which explore the issues of community development and examine some of the myths.

Community Work by Twelvetrees (1991), *You Can't Kill The Spirit* by Miller (1986), a woman's account of her role in the events of the miners' strike in 1984/5, and *What is a Family?* (Development Education Centre 1990) – photographs and activities to get away from the traditional image of the family – are all useful.

So too are *Stolen Childhood* by Vittachi (1989) – looking at children across the world and the pressures on their lives – and *What Teenagers Can Tell Us About Divorce* by Tugendhat (1990).

Learning for Action (Federation for Community Workers/AMA 1990), is a handbook for exercises for encouraging local people to be actively involved in their communities, and *Community Groups Handbook* by Pearse and Smith (1990), offers practical advice to community groups.

All Winners No Losers (YWCA 1989) is a discussion pack, while *Discoveries* published by the YWCA,[2] is a board game looking at a very wide range of beliefs and values with questions to be discussed by groups of young people.

---

2   Available from YWCA Headquarters, Clarendon House, 52 Cornmarket Street, Oxford OX1 3EJ.

POVERTY

Dialogue may include:

- Why are some people, areas, and countries rich, and others poor?
- What does poverty mean to poor people?
- Is poverty an inevitable consequence of living in a free market/competitive/capitalist society?
- What sorts of images do we have of poor people?
- Is charity the only way to relieve poverty?
- What sort of power are people left with when they live in poverty?

...what sort of power are people left with when they live in poverty?

Resources may include *Society Today* by Williams (1986) and *Power and Society* by Dye (1989). These are both basic sociology texts which give clear descriptions in sociological terms of many areas that relate to poverty.

Leaving Home by Dearling and Clark (1985), and *A Place of My Own* by Anne Masterson (1982), look at poverty facing young people who are homeless. Both are well illustrated with accounts from young people.

Young Gifted and Broke by Terry Potter (1989), offers research into young people and low pay, while the *New Internationalist* looks at poverty and its causes and effects in many parts of the world.

THE ENVIRONMENT

Dialogue may include:

- Is environmental damage the inevitable result of the way we organise our society?
- How important are natural resources?
- Why are they in decline?
- Is it related to consumerism?
- Pollution.
- The ozone layer.
- Global warming.
- Rain forests.
- Rivers and rain.
- What are the government's attitudes and responsibilities to the environment?

Resources may include *Earth Works* (Rogers 1990), a teaching pack for young people which looks at all aspects of the environment; *New Internationalist*, which has discussed many environmental issues; and newspapers and journals for up-to-the-minute current affairs.

DISABILITY

Dialogue may include:

- What terms do you think should be used?
- Does it matter?
- What is disability?

- What is the difference between mental and physical disability?
- How do people's surroundings disable them?
- Why do more disabled people live in poverty?
- How are communications made difficult by disabilities?
- How do politicians see disability?
- What places are not accessible to people with disabilities?
- How is an individual's education affected if they have a disability?

Resources may include material from SCOPE (formerly the Spastics Society) – an excellent source of information on cerebral palsy. They have posters, videos, factual information and other material. The *Open University Disability Pack* (Dant and Quinn 1990b), designed to form a short course, is very expensive but worth borrowing from the library. *My Left Foot* by Christy Brown (1990), or the film of the book, is useful to generate discussion and build dialogue.

Managing Disability at Work by Brenda Smith, Margery Povall and Michael Floyd (1991), is useful, and *Know Me As I Am* by Dorothy Atkinson and Fiona Williams (1990), offers prose and poetry by people with learning difficulties and reflects the way people with learning difficulties experience their lives.

Stand up, the Real Glynn Vernon, available from SCOPE,[3] is a useful video which films Glynn Vernon talking about and carrying out his life. *Call Us By Our Name: A Pack about People with Special Learning Needs Resulting from Mental Handicaps* (Community Service Volunteers 1991), and *Disability Awareness* by the Disabled Living Foundation (1989), are also useful.

THE DEVELOPING WORLD

Dialogue may include:

- What is the third world?
- What is a developing country?
- What is the North–South divide?
- Population.

---

3   For details, please write to SCOPE, 12 Park Crescent, London W1N 4EQ.

- How much economic aid is given and what strings are attached.
- What role do multinational companies play in the developing world?

...what role do multi-nationals play...?

- Literacy levels in the developing world and the first world.
- The distribution of poverty around the world.
- How do charities try to help the developing world?
- How this country exploits other countries.
- How this country is exploited.
- Pollution and land exhaustion.
- How cash crops are produced for export from the same country where people are starving.
- Imperialism of the North over the South.
- Can the developing world survive and grow in our capitalist system.

- How much does the fulfilling of our desires for consumer goods depend on the developing world remaining poor?
- The continued existence of slavery.
- How different organisations are trying to change things.
- What is the difference between a freedom fighter and terrorist?

Resources may include *New Internationalist*, and information from 'Red Nose Day' and other massive fund raisers, which can be used to look at how charity events portray those people they are 'helping'.

Oxfam Education[4] has numerous publications which are cheap and designed for use with young people, and look at a wide range of issues affecting the third world. Their catalogue is essential and the following are recommended:

- *Changing Places*
- *Debt Disasters in the Classroom*
- *Economics for Change*
- *Go Bananas*
- *Investigating Images*
- *Land, Poverty and Power*
- *Missing Links*
- *Teaching Development Issues*
- *World in a Supermarket Bag*
- *Where Has All the Food Gone?*

Training for Transformation (Hope, Timmel and Hodzi 1984), three volumes of information and exercises based on the work of Paulo Freire, is cheap and essential, and Latin America Bureau Publications[5] produce a range of material looking at issues affecting Latin America and the Caribbean.

---

4   For details please contact Youth and Education Programme, Oxfam, 274 Banbury Road, Oxford OX2 7DZ.
5   1 Amwell Street, London EC1R 1UL.

HEALTH

Dialogue may include:

- All sorts of things about HIV/AIDS.
- Why do some people use drugs?
- Why do some people use solvents.
- Pregnancy.
- Abortion.
- Contraception.
- Smoking.
- Alcohol.
- Diet.
- Stress.
- The connection between poverty and health.
- Mental health.
- The NHS.
- Doctors.
- Hospitals.
- Eating disorders.
- Sexual abuse.

Resources may include *Our Bodies Ourselves*, edited by Angela Phillips and Jill Rakusen (1989), a big expensive book which gives accurate and comprehensive information on all aspects of women's health. *Women and Health* (Curran, Pleaner and Black 1989), is a handbook of exercises for use with women.

About Adults as Abused Children by Hallum (1987), is a leaflet which raises some of the issues which affect young people who have been abused. *Cry Hard and Swim* by Spring (1987), is a personal account of sexual abuse.

The Anorexic Experience by Lawrence (1984) is useful. *Talking About Health* by Christine Beeles and Penny Mares (1989) and *Health* by Dady (1990), offer collections of exercises designed for use with young women.

The Facts About Adolescent Drug Abuse by Davies and Coggins (1991), provides useful information which gives a realistic picture of the risks that, young people take without undue panic. *Bullying* by La Fountaine

(1991), gives the results of research carried out from the Childline bullying line, and *Go Ask Alice* (Anon 1971) offers a personal account of drug abuse.

Let's Discuss AIDS by Wilkinson (1987), and *Not Just Another AIDS Video* by Avid Productions/Leicester City Council,[6] and *Your Choice For Life*, (Department of Education and Science 1987) are all important.

Posters Alter Attitudes to AIDS by Liverpool Health Promotion Unit (1992) provides good colourful posters which generate discussion, and *Opinions: A Game for Young People On the Issues Around AIDS/HIV*, published by Riverside Health Authority[7] (1988) is helpful.

Letters to Teenagers (YWCA Bristol), records young women's accounts of being pregnant.

Handbook for Young Mothers by Peck (1990) (copies free to young women) provides practical information for young women with children. See also *Too Close For Comfort* by Hayward and Carlyle (1991).

Abortion and Afterwards by Davies (1991) gives accounts by women who have had an abortion. and *Time of the Month* from Youth Clubs UK[8] is a board game for young women about health and sexuality.

SEXUALITY

Dialogue may include:

- Acceptance of people with a different sexuality.
- Recognition of the existence of different forms of sexuality.
- How much a person's sexuality affects the sort of relationships they have with others.
- How people who are not heterosexual are treated.
- How people with different sexualities are mistreated by society.
- Heterosexuality, homosexuality and bisexuality.
- What being homosexual, heterosexual or bisexual means.
- Why some forms of sexuality are considered normal.

---

6   For details please contact Avid Productions, Keswick House, 30 Peacock Lane, Leicester LE5 1NY.

7   For details please write to Kensington, Chelsea and Westminster Health Promotion Unit, 88–94 Westbourne Grove, London W2 5RZ.

8   Available from 11 Bide Street, London EC4A 4AS.

- Does your sexuality affect your ability to work in certain jobs?
- How does the media treat different forms of sexuality?
- Are our stereotypes or images of people with a different sexuality right
- Are we taught to be heterosexual?

Resources may include *The Mirror Within* by Dickson (1985), an honest look at women's sexuality and how it is affected by socialisation. *Not Just a Passing Phase*, edited by the Lesbian History Group (1989) takes a look at some famous lesbians from the past; and *Section 28*, by the Stop the Clause Education Group (1989) looks at the legislation and how to work effectively on sexuality issues despite Clause 28.

Man's World, A Game for Young Men, from B Team Productions[9] and *The Grapevine Game* from Youth Work Press[10] (1991) may be useful. *The Him Book* compiled and illustrated by Chris Meade (1987) provides exercises concentrating on male sexuality, and *Boys Will Be...? Sex Education and Young Men* by Davidson (1990) takes a close look at male sexuality and the detrimental effect it can have on the lives of both boys and girls.

RACISM

Dialogue may include:

- Racial abuse and violence.
- The effects of racism on black people.
- The effects of racism on white people.
- The advantages of a multiracial society.
- Race, employment and unemployment.
- Fascist groups and the Anti Nazi League.
- Hitler and Nazism.
- Images of black people.
- Images of Irish people.

---

9   Available from Flat 2, 120 Marlbourgh Road, Oxford or from the B Team, BCM B Team, London WC1N 3XX.

10   Available from National Youth Agency, 17–23 Albion Street, Leicester LE1 6SD.

- Black people who should be famous.
- How the media portrays black people.

Resources may include *Searchlight*, the newspaper of the Anti Nazi League, which provides good information and counters the claim that it is all a joke and not harmful to anyone.

The Journal reports news from a black perspective and redresses the balance of lack of news regarding black people and issues. Also useful *Anti Racist Resources* by Massil and Rosenberg (1988).

Black History for Beginners by Dennis and Willmarth (1984) is an excellent book, full of information, very readable, with cartoons. *Patterns of Racism* and *The Fight Against Racism*, (Institute for Race Relations 1986a, b) are full of photographs and easily understood information about the history of racism in this country.

Learning in Terror (Commission for Racial Equality 1988), records research into how racism in schools affects young black people's ability to learn. *Teaching Against Prejudice and Stereotyping* by Evans (1988) provides useful ideas for tackling racism with young people. *Beyond the Steel Bands and Samosas* by Chauhan suggests ways of approaching effective antiracist work with young people.

Right of Way (Asian Women's Writing Workshop 1988) is a collection of writing by Asian Women about their experiences of living in this country. *White Lies* (1986) comes from Swingbridge Video,[11] and *Hamari Rangily Zuindagi (Our Colourful Lives)* by Jamagni (1980) records young Asian women talking about themselves.

Images: A Resource Pack (Woodcraft Folk 1987) and *Roots of Racism* (Institute for Race Relations 1982) are also useful.

GENDER

Dialogue may include:

- The different roles played by males and females.
- Why do men and women carry out specific roles?
- What is expected of boys and girls?
- What is it like to be male or female?

---

11   Available from 10a Bridge Street, Gateshead, Tyne and Wear NE8 2EH.

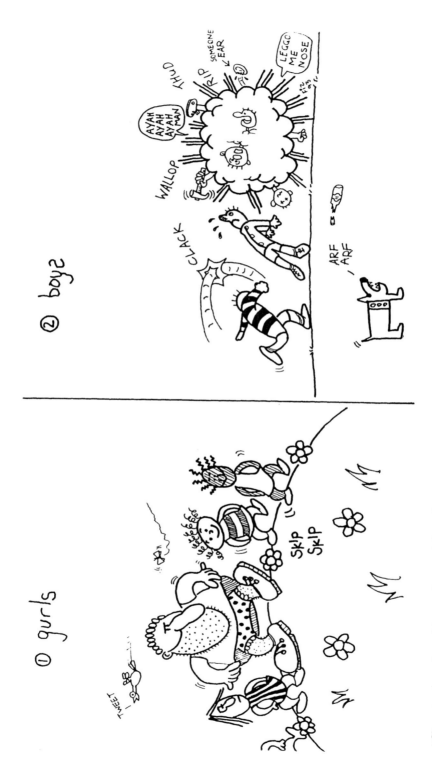

...different roles played by males and females...

- Women who ought to be famous.
- For whose interests does sexism exist?
- Arguments used to justify sexism.
- Benefits of living in a non-sexist world.
- Violence against women.
- Employment issues related to gender.

Resources may include the *Anti Sexist Work with Boys* series (Whyld, Pickersgill and Jackson 1990), which includes a number of booklets all concentrating on exercises and ideas for work with boys, and is a useful cheap and resource. *Greater Expectations* by Szsirom and Dyson (1986) an excellent resource for work with girls and offers exercises for all occasions.

The Him Book (Meades 1987) is again a very cheap but useful resource with a series of exercises for work with boys, and *A Woman in Your Own Right* by Dickson (1982) is accepted as one of the best texts on assertiveness for women, good on its own or as a source of ideas for your own sessions with women. *The Livewire Book of Women Achievers* by Murphy (1990) is also useful.

Just Like a Girl by Sharpe (1976), *There's a Good Girl* by Grabruckner (1988), and *What Society Does to Girls* by Nicholson (1977) all look at sex stereotyping and raise many issues which will generate endless dialogue.

Sexual Harassment in Schools by Herbert (1992) is a valuable survey, while *The Equaliser* (Bread Youth Project 1991) presents more equal opportunities exercises and some excellent ideas for sessions.

Springboard by Willis and Daisley (1990) is useful, as is *Lifting the Limits* by Mountain (1990) for working with young women and *Getting Started* by Harding for good advice on setting up a girls' group.

True to Life (Hemmings 1986) presents writing by young women and *Coming in from the Margins* by Carpenter and Young (1986) is an excellent text on girls' work and its importance to youth work and young people. *You Worry Me Tracy, You Really Do* by Martin (1987a) is a book of cartoons aimed at young women, and a good informal resource.

Girls' Work Unit Newsletters was produced ten years ago by Youth Clubs UK who had a separate girls' work unit, which as well as doing many things to promote work with girls published a bimonthly newsletter packed with information, advice, and details of work being carried out. It was closed and the work was incorporated into the main work of Youth Clubs UK. However, nothing has ever taken its place and if you are lucky enough to be able to get hold of copies, use them, since they are still relevant ten years on...unfortunately.

10 Working with a Group

If you have read the previous sections you will remember that we identified six things that affect the way that groups work. These were: aims, roles, relationships, decisions, communication, and norms. We also discussed how these should be if we are to be most effective in our group work. They were as follows.

1. **Relationships are such that:**
   - people feel part of a group
   - there is respect between the members
   - there is a high degree of trust.

2. **Norms are such that:**
   - everyone is accountable
   - discussion is acceptable
   - actions are justifiable
   - individuals take responsibility
   - all members are entitled to equal participation
   - they are clear.

3. **Aims are such that:**
   - they appeal to all members
   - they are agreed upon
   - they are clear

4. Roles are such that:

- people feel comfortable in them
- they are challenged by them
- they are valued
- the youth worker's role is understood.

5. Decisions are such that:

- everyone has a say in them
- they are not divisive.

6. Communication is such that:

- it is open
- it is respectful
- everyone can participate
- people listen as well as speak.

It is useful to keep all this in mind, as a vision and also as an aid to diagnosing what is going right and wrong.

In most circumstances the youth worker will also be working with the members of the group on an individual basis. This needs to complement and reinforce the work that goes on in the group as much as possible. The following section looks at particular issues that may arise as part of the process of working with a group.

CLARIFYING AIMS

(getting everyone to see where the group is going)

Introduction

Groups need an aim! After all, for many groups the aim is the only reason for their existence, and there seems to be a strong link between the clarity of the aim and the efficiency and effectiveness of the group.

The aim is the main motivational factor in a group, so affirming and clarifying it is time well spent, and a commitment to a single common aim will concentrate energy towards that aim and away from conflicts and distractions.

A clarity of aim means that all members have a clear understanding of what it is that the group is trying to achieve. Within any aim there are secondary aims which may be more or less important to different members of the group, but they all have to understand the common aim. For example, a group may want to organise a concert. The first thing is that everyone has to agree on the type of concert. Brass bands? Punk bands? Free? Profit making? Which one, or which combination, is going to be the primary aim that pulls together the group and which ones are going to be the secondary aims which may only apply to one individual. Even when this is decided, there may be some members who are doing it because they want to perform, whilst others want to make money. These are perfectly reconcilable if everyone agrees on and understands the same overall aim, and this clarification needs to go on throughout the project.

Things to Do and Talk About

- Try to distinguish between the primary and secondary aims.
- Write out aims, ask questions to clarify, and draw up a statement of aims that everyone agrees on.
- Make sure that members can identify with the aim; it may need to be quite broad to incorporate all the individual aims.
- Bring in photographs, maps, books and so on as often as possible, so that there gradually develops a common image of the aim.
- Invite people who have done this sort of project before, especially other young people, to talk to the group.
- Play the devil's advocate and ask questions about the aim, and get people to visualise and shape it.
- Include the development of the skills as one of the aims and sessions on particular subjects.
- Discuss what it will be like when the project aim is met.
- Discuss the skills being one of the aims.
- Arrange activities that act as tasters to the main aim.
- Talk about the primary and secondary aims.
- Talk about times when they might have done something similar before.

GENERATING IDEAS

(coming up with good schemes)

...generating ideas...

Introduction

Ideas for projects that groups want to undertake are sometimes very hard to find. It is quite possible to work with a group for years before an idea emerges that will create the amount of enthusiasm and commitment needed to carry through a project, and an idea that is really yours and you have sold to them is unlikely to generate much commitment and enthusiasm.

Groups do not usually come up with ideas because they are not used to the idea of thinking about what they would do themselves. The ideas may be there, but need 'teasing out' or 'unveiling'.

There is no harm in starting out on a project even if a group might not finish it, as long as the disappointment does not become too negative, although it is worth continuing as long as the benefits of participating outweigh the potential disadvantages of not succeeding with it. It is also important that they arrive at a project that is achievable but will still present a challenge. Perhaps split an over ambitious project into two parts.

Things to Do and Talk About

- Talk about things that other groups have done.
- Ask what they would do if they had £1000.
- Ask what they would do if they won the pools.
- Ask what they want to be doing in one year.
- Ask what they have always wanted to do.
- Ask what they have seen on *Blue Peter*, *In At The Deep End* or *Jim'll Fix It*.
- Ask the group to list ways in which they can find out ideas, e.g. from friends, from relatives, from libraries, from TV, from things they do already, from holidays, from fantasies.
- Reminisce about what they have done before that was good.
- Ask for suggestions of things that would be really boring, and select the things that make them boring; then use this list to shape what they shouldn't be, and build on this to say what they should be.
- Take the group to visit other projects.
- Brainstorm, and to be successful ensure that the problem or question is talked about a little first, that ideas are not judged until afterwards, and that every idea is written down for all to see.

Examples

Trips, discos, motorbike riding, playschemes, back yards, sound rooms, videos, coffee bars, outdoor activities, photography, silk screen printing, plays, making records, learning about computers, competitions (pool, football), credit unions, mother and toddler groups, volunteering, conservation projects, information/notice boards, newsletters, exchanges, tracing family trees, pantomimes, holidays, community history, music making, making toys for playgroups, building wheelchair access, nature trails, camping, barbecues, assault courses, puppets, murals, dances, fanzines, tapeslide shows, food coops, cooking, clothes making, drama, workshops/learning, pet clubs, film shows, exhibitions, bulk buy coops, circuit training, community newspapers, banger projects, radio programme making, puppetry, assault courses, archery, rock climbing, orienteering, skating, canoeing, sailing, water skiing, caving...

MAINTAINING INTEREST

(keeping the enthusiasm going, stickability)

Introduction

Almost all projects go through ups and downs; the ups tend to come when there is a lot being achieved and the tasks are interesting, the downs when the going is slow and the tasks are boring. Enthusiasm can drop off over one session or over the whole project – either way, the same sort of reasons apply. The more the project is the group's idea, the more commitment there will be.

Things to Do and Talk About

- Can the timetable be adjusted so that you don't get long stretches of boring tasks?
- At the beginning of the project get everyone to score out of ten what their chances are of seeing the project through. Then ask what would need to be changed to up each person's score by one point, and what could happen to reduce each person's score by one point. Add up the total score and total possible, and list the things that must happen to bump up each person's score. Repeat the exercise every few sessions. This can also give you an idea of individual feelings about the project.
- Write letters to each person reminding them of the time of the next meeting and what tasks they have got to do for it.
- Give people lifts to meetings.
- Get a minibus and meet at another venue – a change is as good as a rest!
- Keep bringing in books, photographs or anything that will keep the aim fresh in their minds.
- Discuss dropping the project.
- Discuss having a two-week break.

- Consider the aim of the project, what it will be like, what fun it will be.

CLARIFYING ROLES

(who do they think you are? what do they think you will do? are you going to play a role that they have come across before?)

Introduction

'role (rol), n. Actor's part; one's task or function. [foll.]'

(Concise Oxford Dictionary)

It is essential that everyone is clear about the role of the youth worker since it can fundamentally affect the way the group works. Above all, the participants need to understand that it is their project and they are responsible for it. If this is clear, they are far more likely to accept responsibility.

It is a difficult role to explain because most young people have not experienced such a role before. They will have come across authority roles such as teachers or parents and youth leaders who all take a more directive role, but probably not that of a facilitator. One way that this can be clarified is by explaining that you want them to exercise the core skills, and that this will only happen if they are in control of the project. Use this to lead into a discussion of what help you are prepared to give. Above all, remember that people judge what your role is by the way you act.

Be careful to let the group make its own decisions wherever possible, and make sure that when you have to intervene, you try to obtain the group's agreement, since it is no use telling them that they have to make all the decisions if you then keep telling them what decision they have to reach.

Part of your role is likely to include setting the boundaries so whilst you may want to leave them to make their own choices, they should understand that there are boundaries within which this can happen. This is discussed on page 151. It is sometimes difficult to work in this way with a group if they have known you in a different and more directive role before, at there can be too many expectations to overcome.

Things to Do and Talk About

- Discuss the statement 'I am a sports coach and can help you prepare, but you have to go out and actually do it'.
- Discuss 'I can only help you to do everything yourselves'.
- Talk about roles and how the group sees you, using examples of roles such as uncle/aunt, sister/brother, mother/father, teacher, the police.
- Consider what sort of things you would and would not do.
- Discuss what you would expect them to do and what they expect you to do.
- Leave the meeting while a crucial decision is being made, as this emphasises that it is their decision. Use an excuse such as 'I must make a quick phone call'.
- Use contracts and agreements – they can be a useful medium for clarifying your role. This is discussed on page 148.
- Make sure you actually act like a youth worker.
- If being a youth worker means that you are not a leader and the group has to find its own path, then you shouldn't expect to sit at the head of the meeting, or on a higher chair.
- Look at yourself in a session, and consider if you are playing the part of a youth worker or a leader.
- Ask yourself if you are you asking questions or giving answers.

DEALING WITH AWKWARD MEMBERS

(coping with people who cause hassle)

Introduction

All groups have awkward members, who while not intolerable, require a little more attention to contribute to the running of the group. The really important thing to remember is that there has to be a reason why they are behaving as they are. If you can work out this reason, then you are probably half way to solving the problem.

When thinking about awkward members it is worth considering three points.

1. Does his or her behaviour upset you, in what way, and why?

2. Does he or she upset other members of the group, in what way, and why?

3. What, if any, benefit are they deriving from their behaviour?

Under the headings below there are suggestions why people might be the way they are and some ways that youth workers have tackled them. Don't think that it is an exhaustive list, but it might help you work out the reason for the behaviour of people in the group, and how to tackle it.

Rarely will anyone fit neatly into one category. It is more likely that they will be a mixture of several.

Most of the list has been taken from *Training for Transformation* by Hope, Timmel and Hodzi (1984), a handbook for community workers in Zimbabwe.

Member Types:

1. **The donkey,** who is very stubborn, will not change his or her point of view.
    - Do they see changing their mind as a sign of weakness?
      - Talk about the courage needed to admit you are wrong.
    - Do they find it difficult to admit they are wrong?
      - Try to avoid letting them state their point of view until everyone else has spoken and all the information has been made available.
      - Talk about the importance of consensus decisions.

2. **The lion,** who gets in fights whenever others disagree with his or her plans or interfere with his or her desires.
    - Do they think it is a sign of weakness to accept others' ideas?
      - Talk about the courage needed to let others have their way.
    - Do their plans include something that is very important to them?
      - Get everyone to choose the things within the project that they really want to do themselves, then negotiate who gets what.

Do they think it is a sign of weakness?

- ◦ Talk about decision making, how it's to be done, and what is going to happen to the project if decisions can't be made to everyone's satisfaction.
- ◦ Include in the contract, (see page 148) that everyone has to accept decisions, and talk about what this might mean to each individual.

3. **The rabbit,** who runs away as soon as he or she senses tension, conflict, or an unpleasant job. This may mean quickly switching to another topic.

   - • Are they afraid of being blamed for what goes wrong?
     - ◦ Talk about the group taking responsibility for things going wrong.

- Do they always get landed with the unpleasant jobs?
  - When allocating tasks, get the group to share out unpleasant ones equally.
  - Get the group to think about how they are going to deal with stress and tension.
  - Ask the rabbit to take the role of warning the group when there is some tension.

4. **The ostrich,** who buries his or her head in the sand and refuses to face reality or admit there is any problem at all.
   - Are they afraid of things going wrong?
     - Talk about things that have gone wrong in other groups.
     - Talk about what would be the worst thing that could go wrong and what the result of that would be. Would it be as bad as all that?

5. **The monkey,** who fools around, chatters a lot, and prevents the group from concentrating on any serious business.
   - Are they seeking attention?
     - Get them to keep the minutes.
     - Ask them to keep quiet during the meeting but to give a summary at the end of this meeting and at the beginning of the next one.
   - Are they really interested in the group's aim?
     - Talk about how important the aim is to everyone.
     - Talk about how the aim will not be achieved if no work gets done – in other words, get the group to put pressure on the monkey.

6. **The elephant,** who simply blocks the way, and stubbornly prevents the group from continuing along the road to their desired goal.
   - Are they really committed to the aim?
     - Talk about the aim.

- Why do they want to block the project? Is the aim something which they really don't agree with?
  - Look for what it is that they really want to do that would make them more positive about the project.

7. **The giraffe,** who looks down on others, and the project in general, feeling 'I am above all this childish nonsense'.
   - Do they think it is a weakness to learn?
     - Find a way to talk about what they have learnt before.
   - Do they think they know it all?
     - Ask them first for solutions to problems and then go on to discuss them.
     - Look at all the tasks that need doing in the project, and see who can do what. Can the giraffe do them all?
     - Talk about who has done a project like this before.
   - Do they think the project is childish?
     - Talk about how rare it is for a group like this to do such an ambitious project.
     - Talk about the fact that the whole group is doing the project and everyone's contribution is important.

8. **The tortoise,** who withdraws from the group, refusing to give his or her opinions.
   - Are they afraid their opinions will be ridiculed?
     - Talk about how some of the most brilliant ideas get ridiculed at first, e.g. the bouncing bomb, and the jet aeroplane.
     - Talk about how important it is that everyone's opinions are taken seriously.
   - Are they insulted because their idea was not accepted?
     - Talk about how everyone has to compromise in a group.

9. **The cat,** who is always looking for sympathy. 'It is so difficult for me...miaow...'

    - Are they unsure that their contribution to the group is of value?
        ◦ Make a point of crediting them with their contributions.
        ◦ Give them plenty of sympathy.
    - Do they have difficulties that others don't, e.g. child care?
        ◦ Ensure that these difficulties are taken into consideration when planning the sessions.

10. **The peacock,** who is always showing off, competing for attention. 'See what a fine person I am'.

    - Do they feel undervalued?
        ◦ Make sure they get credit for things they do.
    - Are they worried they might get left on the sideline?
        ◦ Give them a specific task such as minute taking, or being chairperson.

11. **The rhino,** who charges around putting his or her foot in it, and upsetting people unnecessarily.

    - Are they aware that they are upsetting people?
        ◦ Talk about how important it is that group members feel at ease in the group.
        ◦ Talk about how important it is the group agrees on what actions are needed before they are carried out.
    - Are they over enthusiastic?
        ◦ Talk about how important it is that plans are thought through carefully.
        ◦ Draw up a very detailed task list so everyone knows exactly what they have got to do.

12. **The owl,** who looks very solemn and pretends to be very wise, always talking in long words and complicated sentences.

    - Do they think that their ideas will impress more with long words?
        ◦ Play the devil's advocate and ask what they mean.

- Get everyone to say what they think in one sentence of 20 words.
- Give them extra credit when they say something with short words in clear sentences.

13. **The mouse,** who is too timid to speak up on any issue.
   - Are they afraid their comments will be ridiculed?
     - Try to get an agreement that every comment is taken seriously.
     - Get the group to write down ideas and read out the whole list without saying who wrote which comment.
     - Ensure you give them particular credit for their ideas.
     - Go round the group and ask for one comment each.
   - Are they just naturally quiet?
     - Get them to take minutes so that they can remain quiet, but will not be left out.
     - Find them other tasks to do that do not include much speaking.

14. **The frog**, who croaks on and on about the same subject in a monotonous voice.
   - Get an agreement on the agenda at the beginning and stick to it.
   - Put up a list of comments that have to be kept in mind and make sure that the frog's subject is on it.

15. **The hippo,** who sleeps all the time, and never puts up his head except to yawn.
   - Are they really interested in the aim?
     - Reaffirm the aim.
   - Are they just avoiding contributing because they are worried about how it will be received?
     - Make sure they get credited for what they do.
     - Get them to take minutes to keep them awake.

16. **The cuckoo**, who tries to unsettle all the other eggs in the nest.

- Why are they so keen to put everyone else down?
- Are they doing it before the others get a chance to put them down?
  - Write into the contract 'No put-downs'.
- Are they testing you out to see how far they can go.
  - Make sure that the boundaries are agreed.
  - Talk about the pecking order, who is at the top, who is at the bottom. This can help people to see what is going on in their group.

17. **The parrot,** who talks all the time and doesn't let anyone else get a word in.

- Give everyone three tokens which allow them three opportunities to speak. They cannot speak once they have used them up.
- Get them to take minutes.
- Get them to summarise at the end.

18. **The scapegoat,** who, like the biblical origin of the saying is loaded up with everyone else's guilt and blame, and left in the wilderness.

- Do they like being the scapegoat? In many established groups the scapegoat gets a certain amount of kudos from this role and is quite happy with it, and you may need to accept it to some extent.
  - Try to give the scapegoat credit for things they do.
  - Make sure everyone accepts the blame for things that go wrong.
- Are they the scapegoat because they are lacking in confidence about speaking up and acting for themselves?
  - Give them extra support in their tasks.
  - Make sure they understand their tasks and feel able to carry them out.

It is worth pointing out that many of these problems can be dealt with by:

- Trying not to be offensive to individuals.
- Trying not to put individuals down.
- Trying not to compete with group members.
- Making sure that everyone feels that their contributions are of value.
- Making sure that there is a clear aim.
- Working in pairs or small groups.

It is also important to remember that not all your work has to be done in the group. It is often worthwhile taking one member aside, talking through the problem and winning them over or persuading them to act differently.

INTRODUCING GROUP MEMBERS

(getting to know each other)

Introduction

Introduction games can be difficult. Things are always a bit strained because no one knows each other and everyone is a little apprehensive. Often in project based group work the group already knows each other, but if they don't, an introduction session can help to break the ice. A group will not gel and start to function until people begin to feel at ease with each other.

Things to Do and Talk About

- Discuss almost any sort of activity; the more it allows people to talk and mix, the better.
- Try 'Consequences'. Each member has a paper and pencil. They all write on the top who they are, fold over the top and pass it on one to the left. Then they all write what their hobbies are, once again fold the paper over and pass it on. They repeat the process for what they want to be, what they think of the other members of the group, what they think the group will achieve, and what effect it will have on them. It is always fun reading them out at the end and inevitably there are plenty of good jokes. You should

alter the questions to suit the group, but try to keep them specific so that there is some relationship between the different answers.

- Try throwing a ball to each other and shouting out the name of the person who throws it, or the name of the person who they throw it.
- Try introducing the person on your left; first say what you think they are like and then, after five minutes of chat, what they are really like. A set of preselected questions such as job, age, hobbies, and why in group can help.
- Talk about who already knows who.
- Discuss names and nicknames.

COOPERATING AND TEAM WORK

(pulling together, working as one, hanging together, going hand in hand)

Introduction

It is difficult to isolate the building of cooperation and team work from good group work. The whole essence of good group work is working towards a group that allows people to 'participate on an equal basis'. It means that everyone's contribution is seen to be of value and that the *group* is seen to have achieved the end result and not one, or some, of the individual members.

So building cooperation and team work is something that goes on throughout the project and comes from trust, confidence, respect for other group members, sensitivity and, above all, a recognition that through cooperation more can be achieved. The facilitator can help with this by regularly pointing out how cooperation is getting the results and adding to the enjoyment.

Things to Do and Talk About

- Get each member of the group to choose the five most important features of, for example, a car, that they would like to have and to plan out its use for the next week. Then get the whole group to do it. Discuss how much the individual list and the plan for its use compare with when it was done as a group.

- Get the group members to build a card or domino tower, individually and together. Discuss.
- Many of the group or team exercises in other sections of this manual can be used for cooperation and team building.
- Discuss the skills and talents that group members have between them.
- Ask if any of the individuals have all the skills and talents needed.
- Discuss good examples of team or group success.
- Discuss any successes that the group has achieved through cooperation.

MEETINGS

(times to sort out and plan, confab, coffee time)

Introduction

Meetings are the sessions when the group is all together with the youth worker and it is important that the structure is such that the group can operate at its best. Meetings need to be arranged and structured so that they suit the particular group you are working with, and this could be anything from an informal get together to a chaired and structured meeting. It is not simply a question of deciding how a meeting should run.

You can set the tone from the beginning. Think how differently a group of young people would respond if the first meeting was in a committee room at the civic centre and everyone was provided with a folder, pens, and a name sticker, compared to a first meeting in a corner of a hall in a youth club, sitting on the floor trying to be heard above the noise of a disco. Neither of these ways is wrong or right; each sets a different tone and creates different expectations.

So think about things like the layout of the room, your body language, and the type of people who make up the group. The important thing for you to do is to think how you create the right atmosphere for the group to be at ease, so that the greatest is achieved not just in action but also in skills learning, cooperation, trust and dialogue.

Things to Do and Talk About

- Construct an agenda to which everyone can contribute.
- It sometimes helps groups to concentrate if they know how much needs to be done in what length of time.
- If you don't have a written agenda, you need to be particularly sensitive to members wanting to bring up issues and questions.
- Write the minutes up on a sheet on the wall as you go along
- Describe the agenda as an objective, like 'The objective of this meeting is to deal with the following items... Our aim is by the end of the meeting to have sorted them out to everyone's satisfaction, and to feel that we have achieved and learnt something'.
- Plan for concentration spans.
- Record each week in polaroids and write the agenda on the back.

...plan for concentration spans...

- Record each week in a scrap book which includes the agenda, minutes and relevant documents from the meetings.
- Use flip charts which bring formality but enable everyone to see what is happening.
- Arrange the room for the best results, e.g. in a circle, square, or semicircle with a flip chart in front.
- Suggest that people can only talk if they hold a particular pen which has to be passed around; this brings order to discussion without a chairperson.
- Suggest that people have to pay a token each time they speak, and ensure that they all get a set number to start with.
- Have someone whose task is to remind everyone else what was decided at the last meeting.
- Make sure that everyone gets a say.
- Check that people are not being excluded because of gender, class, race, disability.
- Make sure that the meetings do not waste time.
- Discuss if decisions are being taken with enough thought.
- Ask if we need someone to take charge of meetings.
- Ask if we forget what we talked about last meeting.
- At the end of the session, get someone or everyone to sum up the outcome of the meeting
- Think about feed back – do people stare out of windows, contribute if they want to, drop out, or feel they have achieved something?

CONTRACTS AND AGREEMENTS

(doing a deal, making a pact)

Introduction

There are a number of sections of this manual that argue how important it is that everyone involved in a project has a clear and common understanding of what is going on. Many youth workers find that it is worth trying to draw this up into some sort of contract, either written or verbal. The advantages of this are that:

Contract...either written or verbal

- Everyone knows where they stand.
- The drawing up of the contract can encompass decision making, negotiation, recognition and transference of skills, and a mine of opportunities for dialogue.
- It allows everyone to have an input.
- It assists with planning time and energy.
- It can be useful for evaluation.
- It raises the whole consciousness of the group about the project and process.
- It need not be inflexible but can provide direction and structure.

- It can enable young people to see the project in a different light from before.
- It can help clarify aims, roles, and boundaries.
- It can help you plan the sessions.
- It can lay down a structure for the meetings, i.e. times and duration.
- It makes you as a youth worker partly accountable to the group for your actions.

It can be updated as the project progresses and different issues and problems arise; a contract should never be inflexible if the situation changes. Make sure that you stick to your side of the agreement, as this will encourage the group to adhere to their side and allow them to see that they can trust you.

Things to Do and Talk About

- Discuss what things you might do that would get them really cross.
- Discuss what things would get you really cross.
- Consider what happens if you or they fail to fulfil the contract.
- Ask what they expect of you.
- Discuss contracts at work.

Things that can be Included

- Time, duration, venue, and structure of meetings.
- Youth workers' responsibilities.
- Evaluation method.
- Additional sessions on e.g. racism, sexism, or other related subjects.
- The guarantee of finance if certain targets are achieved.
- Sessions on literacy and numeracy.
- If people decide to drop out, they should tell the group or facilitator why.
- No put-downs such as 'I won't make you feel bad if you won't make me feel bad'.
- Special agreements with specific individuals.

- Project rules.
- Time commitments from the facilitator and participants.
- The aim of the group.

You can get everyone to sign the contract after it has been drawn up.

INTERVENING

(putting your foot down, setting the limits, a licence to step in)

...a licence to step in...

Introduction

There are a number of reasons why youth workers might have to intervene. They are based on:

- Legal grounds.
- Administrative grounds, e.g. fire or insurance regulations.
- Moral or ethical grounds (see value base).

- The group making serious errors (i.e. those from which they might not be able to recover, or those which could jeopardise their project).

- Setting boundaries, i.e. setting out the limits of behaviour that you are prepared to tolerate. All youth workers need to set boundaries over which young people cannot step. Often young people will continue to test you out until these are clear. You will already do this in your youth work and there is no reason that the same boundaries should not apply to the groups as well.

Things to Do and Talk About

- Discuss what sort of things they are not prepared to tolerate from you.
- Discuss what you are not prepared to tolerate from them.
- Explain very carefully why you are putting you foot down.
- Write the limits and boundaries into the contract.
- Tell them that there is some reason why they cannot do what they are planning, and ask them to work out what the reason is.

If the group does not understand why you are stopping them from doing something, they will no longer feel they are in control. They are entitled to challenge you on your interventions.

DROPPING A PROJECT

(enough is enough, no point in going on)

Introduction

In any piece of work there is a point at which it is no longer worth continuing. In the case of project based groupwork it should be the point at which the skills are no longer being exercised and dialogue is not getting built. This can be a tortuous decision because many workers are under pressure from the management, peers, or personal pride to produce the goods and continue with projects.

It is important then that you educate yourself, your peers and management to understand what project based group work is about. If you decide that a project has to fold, then this may well be a good opportunity to do this. You may decide that even though the skills are not being exercised and dialogue is not being built, it is still worth going on. This is okay because sometimes projects are worth completing for other reasons than skill development. Your management group may be expecting it, other young people may be expecting it, someone may be depending on it. However, in these circumstances, this book will be less use to you.

Things to Do and Talk About

- Carry out the scoring method from page 79.
- Build into the contract the point at which the project will fold.
- Look at the section on finishing projects.
- Consider how much you really want to do the project.
- Talk about thinking of another project.

11 Planning and Finishing Off Your Project

PLANNING

Even before you start talking to groups about doing a project, it is worth having some sort of plan in your mind. Below is a list of things you might want to consider in your plan.

1. **First stage** (preparing the ground)
   - Does your management group or officer understand what you are trying to do?
   - Do you colleagues understand what you are trying to do?
   - How are you going to evaluate your own performance?
   - How are you going to arrange the meetings?
   - Do you have access to the sort of resources you might need to build dialogue?
   - Have you got some time set aside to plan and think about the project?
   - Where is your group coming from?

2. **Second stage** (getting the group together)
   - How are you going to explain the skills to the group?
   - What atmosphere do you want to cultivate?
   - How are you going to explain your role?
   - How are you going to break the ice?

- How are you going to get the group to evaluate at the end?
- How are you going to get the group to gel?
- What boundaries are you going to set?

3. **Third stage** (getting the project thought through)
    - What issues would you like to build a dialogue about?
    - How are you going to clarify the aim?
    - Where is the idea for the project going to come from?
    - Are you going to draw up a contract or agreement with the group?
    - Can you build in assessing strengths and weaknesses?
    - Can you build in making decisions?
    - Can you build in negotiation?
    - Can you plan sessions so that there is time for both activity and dialogue?

4. **Fourth stage** (planning the project)
    - Can you build in assessing strengths and weaknesses?
    - Can you build in seeking information and advice?
    - Can you build in making decisions?
    - Can you build in planning time and energy?
    - What opportunities might arise for building dialogue?

5. **Fifth stage** (implementing the project)
    - Do participants recognise the skills they are developing?
    - Are participants able to evaluate how they are doing?
    - Are the skills getting covered?
    - Can you build in carrying through agreed responsibilities?
    - Can you build in negotiation skills?
    - Can you build in dealing with people in power and authority?

6. **Sixth stage** (finishing off)

   - How are the participants going to evaluate their performance?
   - Will the group disperse or do another project?
   - Are there any follow up pieces of work you need to do? Are there any other directions that the group or the individuals want to follow up, e.g. further education, community groups?
   - How do you evaluate your work?

7. **Throughout**

   - How can you ensure that the participants value the skills?
   - How can you ensure that the participants recognise they have improved and can improve the skills?
   - Can you build in problem solving?
   - Can you build in resolving conflicts?

   - Can you build in coping with stress and tension?
   - Can you build in communication?

8. **Problems**

   - Are you having difficulty with individuals in the group?
   - Is the group losing interest?
   - Should you drop the project?
   - Do you need to put your foot down about something?
   - Can you ensure that the group operates effectively?
   - How can you ensure that you don't become the leader?

FINISHING OFF

Although a project is coming to an end, it does not mean that the development of the group members is concluding. Facilitators should be thinking of what the participants are going to do now, and how to give the project an appropriate ending.

...finishing off a project...

There are three things that are worth considering.

1. What are they going to do now?

    - Further education? Have any members expressed any interest in pursuing anything they have been doing?
    - Another project? This needs to be a challenge.
    - Do they think they could take their skills further and try to create change?

2. How are they going to look back on the project?

   - Have a party or night out to celebrate the completion of their project.
   - Run off some copies of the scrapbook for everyone to take away.

3. What cropped up during the project that needs further work?

References

Anon (1971) *Go Ask Alice*. London: Corgi.

Asian Women's Writers' Workshop (eds) (1988) *Right of Way*. London: The Women's Press.

Atkinson, D. and Williams, F. (1990) *Know Me As I Am*. Sevenoaks: Hodder and Stoughton.

Beeles, C. and Mares, P. (1989) *Talking About Health*. London: Health Education Authority.

Bread Youth Project (1991) *The Equaliser*. Bristol: Bread Youth Project (84 Colston Street).

Bronowski, J. (1973) *The Ascent of Man*. London: BBC Books.

Brown, C. (1990) *My Left Foot*. New York, NY: Minerva.

Carpenter, V. and Young, K. (1986) *Coming in from the Margins*. Leicester: National Association of Youth Clubs. (Available from 30 Peacock Lane, Leicester LE1 5NY.)

Chauhan, V. *Beyond the Steel Bands and Samosas*. Leicester: National Youth Agency.

Coles, M.J. and Robinson, W.D. (eds) (1989) *Teaching Thinking: A Survey of Programmes of Education*. Bristol: Bristol Press.

Commission for Racial Equality (1988) *Learning in Terror*. London: Commission for Racial Equality.

Community Links (1989) *Community Links Ideas Annual* Sheffield: Sheffield Women's Printing Co-op. (Available from Community Links, Aizlewoods Mill, Nursery Street, Sheffield S3 8GG.)

Community Links (1990) *Community Links Ideas Annual* Sheffield: Sheffield Women's Printing Co-op. (Available from address above.)

Community Links (1991) *Community Links Ideas Annual* Sheffield: Sheffield Women's Printing Co-op. (Available from address above.)

Community Service Volunteers (1991) *Call Us By Our Name: A Pack about People with Special Learning Needs Resulting from Mental Handicaps*. London: Community Service Volunteers (237 Pentonville Road, London N1).

Curran, M., Pleaner, M. and Black, J. (1989) *Women and Health* London: WEA. (WEA Publications Department, 9 Upper Berkeley Street, London W1H 8BY.)

Dady, B.J. (1990) *Health*. Sevenoaks: Hodder and Stoughton.

Dant, T. and Quinn, G. (1990a) *Disability – Changing Practice* (video). Buckingham: Open University.

Dant, T. and Quinn, G. (1990b) *Open University Disability Pack*. Buckingham: Open University.

Davidson, N. (1990) *Boys Will Be...? Sex Education and Young Men*. London: Bedford Square Press.

Davies, J. and Coggins, N. (1991) *The Facts About Adolescent Drug Abuse*. London: Cassell.

Davies, V. (1991) *Abortion and Afterwards*. Bath: Ashgrove Press.

Dearling, A. and Clark, M. (1985) *Leaving Home*. Glasgow: SITRC (19 Elmbank Street, Glasgow G2 4PB).

Dennis, D. and Willmarth, S. (1984) *Black History for Beginners*. London: Writers' and Readers' Cooperative.

Department of Education and Science (1987) *Your Choice for Life* (book and video). London: AIDS Education/Department of Education and Science.

Development Education Centre (1990) *What is a Family?*. Birmingham: Development Education Centre. (Available from Development Education Centre, Bristol Road, Selly Oak, Birmingham B29 6LE.)

Dickson, A. (1982) *A Woman in Your Own Right*. London: Quartet.

Dickson, A. (1985) *The Mirror Within*. London: Quartet.

Disabled Living Foundation (1989) *Disability Awareness*. London: Disabled Living Foundation.

Dye, T.R. (1989) *Power and Society*. Pacific Grove, CA: Brooks/Cole.

Evans, R. (1988) *Teaching Against Prejudice and Stereotyping*. Oxford: Oxford Development Education Unit.

Federation of Community Workers/AMA (1990) *Learning for Action*. Sheffield: Federation of Community Workers/AMA. (Available from 356 Glossop Road, Sheffield S10 2HW.)

Freire, P. (1970) *Pedagogy of the Opposed*. New York, NY: Continuum.

Freire, P. (1976) *The Practice of Freedom*. London: Writers' and Readers' Publishing Cooperative.

Galbraith, J.K. (1977) *The Affluent Society*. London: André Deutsch.

Grabruckner, M. (1988) *There's a Good Girl*. London: The Women's Press.

Greenaway, R. (1990) *More than Activities*. London: Save the Children.

Hallum, F. (1987) *About Adults as Abused Children*. London: Independent Order of Foresters (36-38 Peckham Road, London SE5 8QR).

Harding, L. *Getting Started*. Leicester: Youth Clubs UK (30 Peacock Lane, Leicester LE1 5NY).

Hayward, J. and Carlyle, D. (1991) *Too Close for Comfort*. Wisbech, Cambs: Learning Development Aids.

Hemmings, S. (ed) (1986) *True to Life*. London: Sheba Feminist Publications.

Herbert, C. (1992) *Sexual Harassment in Schools*. London: David Fulton Publishers.

Hope, A. Timmel, S. and Hodzi, C. (1984) *Training for Transformation*. Zimbabwe: Mambo Press. (Available from CAFOD, 2 Romero Close, Stockwell Road, London SW9 9TY.)

Institute for Race Relations (1982) *Roots of Racism*. London: Institute for Race Relations (2 Lepke Street, London WC1X 9HS).

Institute for Race Relations (1986a) *Patterns of Racism*. London: Institute for Race Relations (as above).

Institute for Race Relations (1986b) *The Fight Against Racism*. London: Institute for Race Relations (as above).

Jamagni, L. (1980) *Hamari Rangily Zuindagi (Our Colourful Lives)*. Leicester: Youth Clubs UK (30 Peacock Lane, Leicester LE1 5NY).

Kuenstler, P. (1960) *The 8th Charles Russell Memorial Lecture – Gangs, Groups and Clubs*. (Publisher not known.)

LaFountaine, J. (1991) *Bullying*. London: Calouste Gulbenkian Foundation (98 Portland Place, London W1N 4ET).

Lawrence, M. (1984) *The Anorexic Experience*. London: The Women's Press.

Lesbian History Group (ed) (1989) *Not Just a Passing Phase*. London: The Women's Press.

Lipman, M. (1988) *Philosophy Goes to School*. Philadelphia: Temple University Press.

Lipman, M. (1991) *Thinking in Education*. Cambridge: Cambridge University Press.

Liverpool Health Promotion Unit (1992) *Posters Alter Attitudes to AIDS*. Liverpool: Liverpool Health Promotion Unit.

Martin, A. (1987a) *You Worry me Tracy, You Really Do!* London: The Women's Press.

Martin, A. (1987b) *He'd Be Quite Nice*. London: The Women's Press.

Martin, A. (1987c) *Even My Gran*. London: The Women's Press.

Massil, G. and Rosenberg, D. (1988) *Anti Racist Resources*. London: The Runnymede Trust (178 North Gower Street, London NW1 2N5).

Masterson, A. (1982) *A Place of My Own.* Leicester: GMYA/National Association of Youth Clubs. (Available from 30 Peacock Lane, Leicester LE1 5NY.)

Meade, C. (ed) (1987) *The Him Book.* Sheffield: Sheffield City Libraries. (Available from the Central Library, Surrey Street, Sheffield S1 1XZ.)

Miller, J. (1986) *You Can't Kill the Spirit.* London: The Women's Press.

Mountain, A. (1990) *Lifting the Limits.* Leicester: National Youth Agency (17-23 Albion Street, Leicester LE1 6SD).

Murphy, K. (1990) *The Livewire Book of Women Achievers.* London: The Women's Press.

New Internationalist (1989) 'Do You Need Treatment?'. November.

Nicholson, J. (1977) *What Society Does To Girls.* London: Virago.

O'Hagan, R. (1991) *The Charnwood Papers.* Ticknall, Derbyshire: Education Now Publishing Cooperative.

Pearse, M. and Smith, J. (1990) *Community Groups Handbook.* London: Journeyman Press.

Peck, F. (1990) *Handbook for Young Mothers.* London: The Rainer Foundation (89 Blackheath Hill, London SE10 8TJ).

Phillips, A. and Rakusen, J. (eds) (1989) *Our Bodies Ourselves.* London: Penguin.

Pirsig, R. (1976) *Zen and the Art of Motorcycle Maintenance.* London: Corgi.

Potter, T. (1989) *Young Gifted and Broke.* Birmingham: West Midlands Low Pay Unit. (Available from Wolverly House, 18 Digbert, Birmingham B5 6BJ).

Quine, W.V. and Ullian, J.S. (1978) *The Web of Belief.* New York, NY: Random House.

Rogers, A. (ed) (1990) *Earth Works.* Reading: Council for Environmental Education, Faculty of Education and Community Studies (University of Reading, London Road, Reading RG1 5AQ).

Rooney, S. (1990) *When People Take the Mickey.* Sevenoaks: Hodder and Stoughton.

Sharpe, S. (1976) *Just Like a Girl.* London: Pelican.

Simons, G. (1989) *Working Together: How to Become More Effective in a Multi-Cultural Organisation.* Los Altos, CA: Crisp Publications.

Smith, B., Povall, M. and Floyd, M. (1991) *Managing Disability at Work: Improving Practice in Organisations.* London: Jessica Kingsley Publishers/Rehabilitation Resource Centre.

Spring, J. (1987) *Cry Hard and Swim.* London: Virago Press.

Stop the Clause Education Group (1989) *Section 28*. London: Stop the Clause Education Group. (Available from Room 216, 38 Mount Pleasant, London WC1X 6AP.)

Szsirom, T. and Dyson, S. (1986) *Greater Expectations*. Wisbech, Cambs: Learning Development Aids.

Tugendhat, J. (1990) *What Teenagers Can Tell Us About Divorce*. London: Bloomsbury.

Twelvetress, A. (1991) *Community Work*. London: Macmillan.

Vittachi, A. (1989) *Stolen Childhood*. Cambridge: Polity Press.

Whyld, J., Pickersgill, D. and Jackson, D. (1990) *Anti Sexist Work with Boys* (series). Carster: Whyld Publishing Co-op (Moorland House, Carster, Lancashire LN7 6SF).

Wilkinson, G. (1987) *Let's Discuss AIDS*. East Sussex: Wayland Publishers.

Williams, M. (1986) *Society Today*. London: Macmillan.

Willis, L. and Daisley, J.. (1990) *Springboard*. Stroud: Hawthorn Press.

Woodcraft Folk (1987) *Images: A Resource Pack*. London: Woodcraft Folk.

YWCA (1989) *All Winners No Losers*. Oxford: YWCA. (Available from YWCA Headquarters, Clarendon House, 52 Cornmarket Street, Oxford OX1 3EJ.)

YWCA Bristol. *Letters to Teenagers*. Bristol: YWCA Bristol (Whitefield Fishponds School, Snowdon Road, Fishponds, Bristol BS16 2HD).

FURTHER READING

General

Jeffs, T. and Smith, M. (eds) (1990) *Using Informal Education*. Buckingham: Open University Press.

Jeffs, T. and Smith, M. (eds) (1990) *Young People, Inequality and Youth Work*. London: Macmillan.

Groups

Bond, T. (1986) *Games for Life and Social Skills*. London: Hutchinson.

Brown, A. (1986) *Groupwork*. Aldershot: Gower.

Douglas, T. (1978) *Basic Groupwork*. London: Tavistock.

Guthrie. E. and Miller, W. S. (1981) *Process Politics*. San Diego, CA: University Associates.

Jennings, S. (1986) *Creative Drama in Groupwork*. Bicester: Winslow Press.

Kindred, M. *Once Upon a Group*. Southwell, Notts: M. Kindred (20 Dover Street, Southwell, Notts NG25 0EZ).

Preston-Shoot, M. (1987) *Effective Groupwork*. Basingstoke: Macmillan Education.

Sanders, G. (1991) *The Pictorial Guide to Group Work Activities*. Available from G. Sanders, 22 New Street, Kenilworth CV8 2EZ.

Evaluation

Everitt, A. Hardiker, P., Littlewood, J. and Mullender, A. (1992) *Applied Research for Better Practice*. London: Macmillan.

Rankin, M. (1986) *Fit a Motor to Your Bike: A Cheap and Easy Training and Evaluation Process for Short Term Funded Project Workers*. Berkhamstead, Herts: Volunteer Centre UK.

Standing Conference of Youth Organisations in Northern Ireland (1984) *Everything O.K.? Review Exercises for Youth Groups*. Belfast: Standing Conference of Youth Organisations in Northern Ireland.

Widlake, P. (1984) *A First Guide to Self-Evaluation for Community Education Workers*. Community Education Development Centre.

Printed in the United Kingdom
by Lightning Source UK Ltd.
130705UK00001B/156/A